"Tell me the last time any book disturbed you. When you give up, buy Uzumaki."
– Warren Ellis

UZUMAKI

Story and Art by JUNJI ITO

SPIRALS... THIS TOWN IS CONTAMINATED WITH SPIRALS...

Kurouzu-cho, a small fogbound town on the coast of Japan, is cursed. According to Shuichi Saito, the withdrawn boyfriend of teenager Kirie Goshima, their town is haunted not by a person or being but by a pattern: uzumaki, the spiral, the hypnotic secret shape of the world. It manifests itself in everything from seashells and whirlpools in water to the spiral marks on people's bodies, the insane obsessions of Shuichi's father and the voice from the cochlea in our inner ear. As the madness spreads, the inhabitants of Kurouzu-cho are pulled ever deeper into a whirlpool from which there is no return!

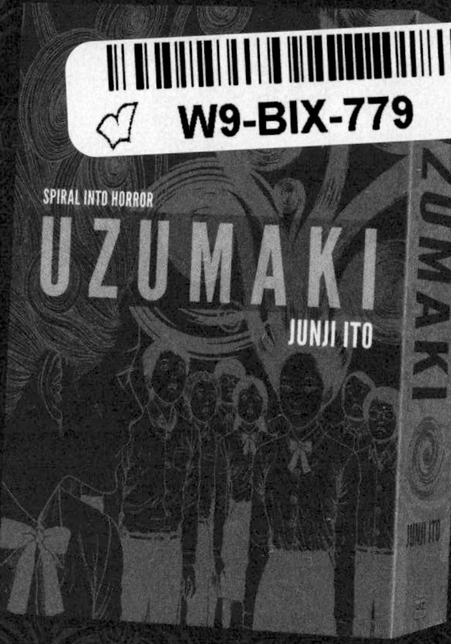

A masterpiece of horror manga, now available in a
DELUXE HARDCOVER EDITION!

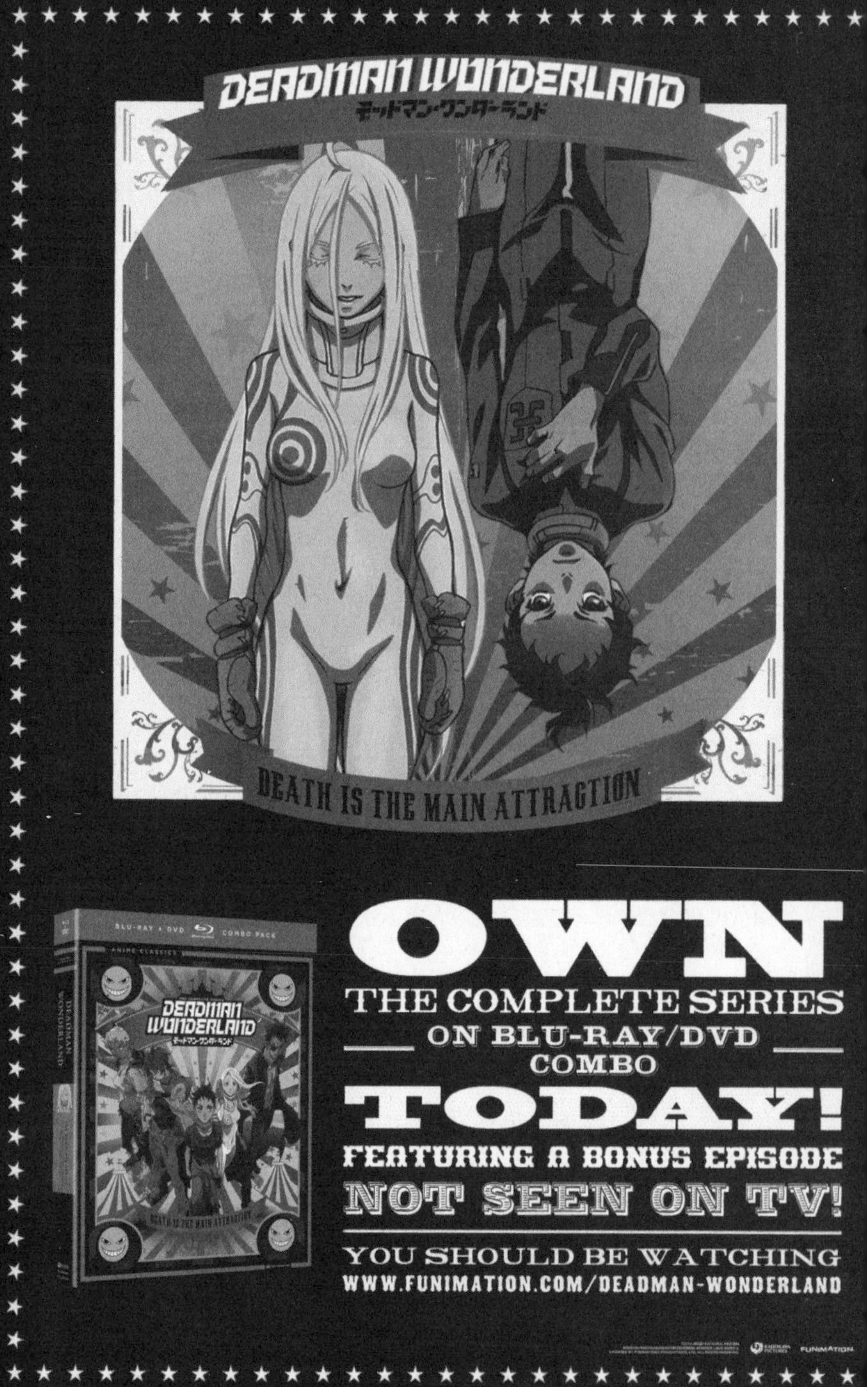
DEADMAN WONDERLAND
デッドマン・ワンダーランド
DEATH IS THE MAIN ATTRACTION
BLU-RAY + DVD COMBO PACK
ANIME CLASSICS
DEADMAN WONDERLAND
OWN
THE COMPLETE SERIES
ON BLU-RAY/DVD
COMBO
TODAY!
FEATURING A BONUS EPISODE
NOT SEEN ON TV!
YOU SHOULD BE WATCHING
WWW.FUNIMATION.COM/DEADMAN-WONDERLAND
FUNIMATION

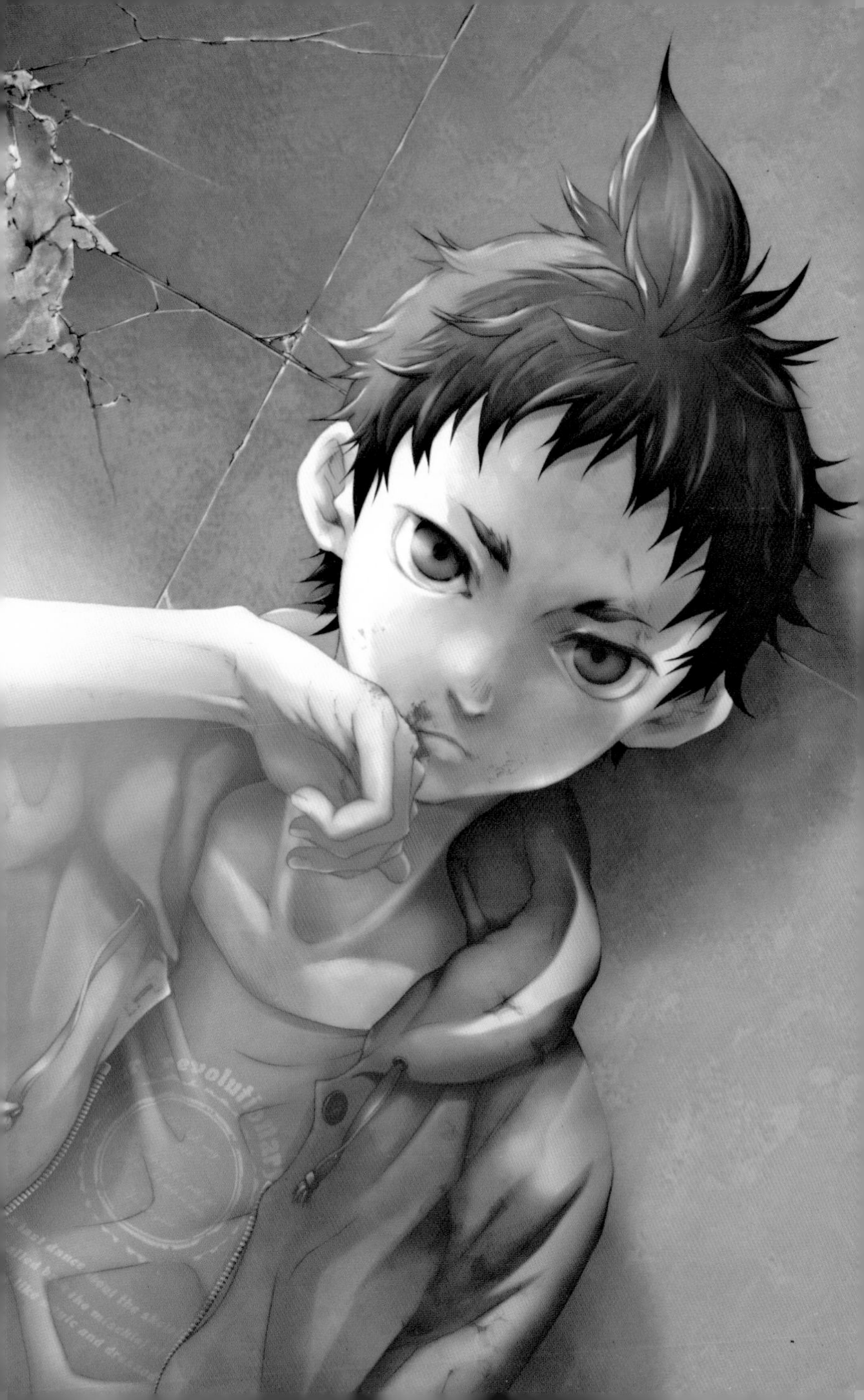

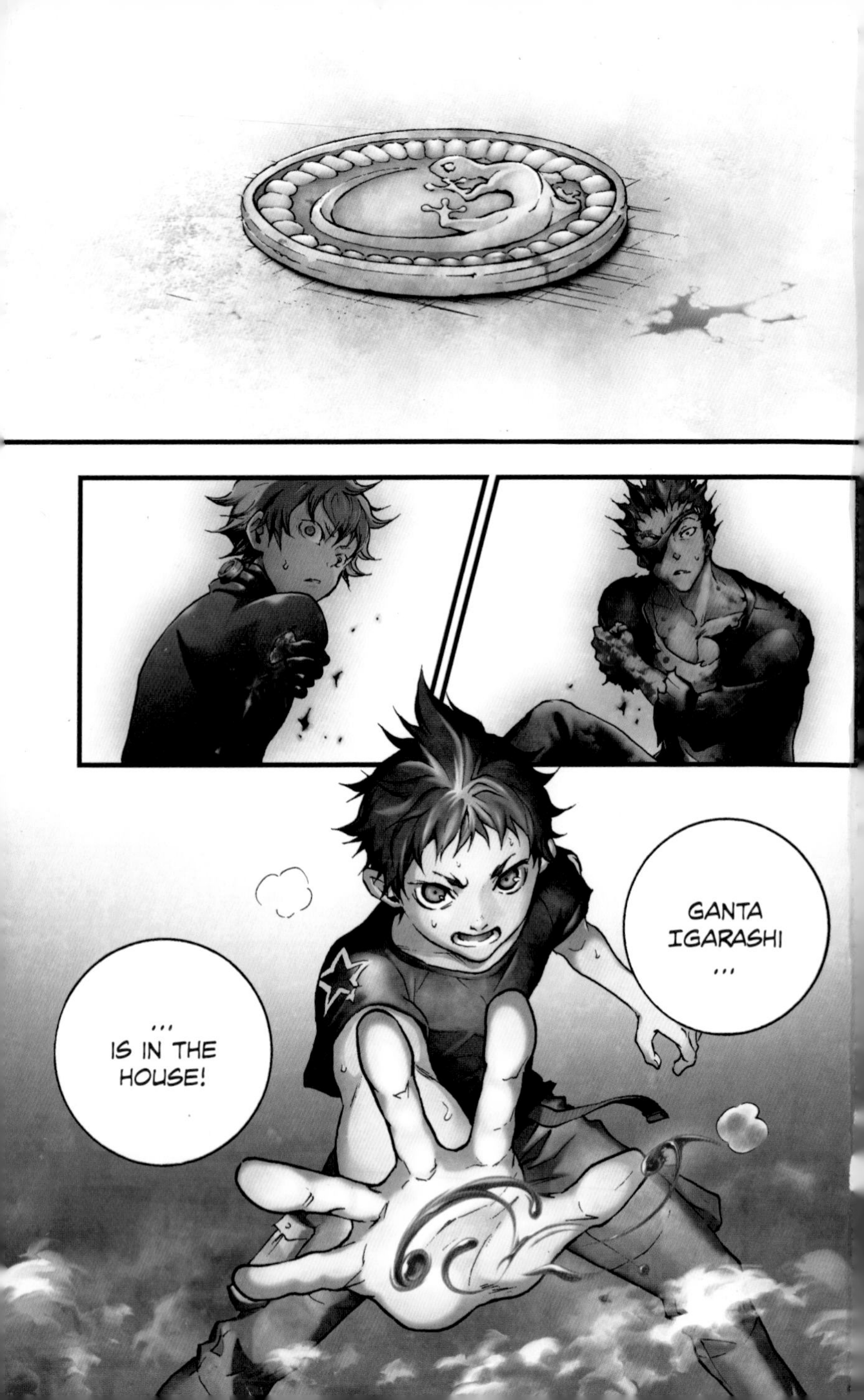
GANTA IGARASHI ...
... IS IN THE HOUSE!

DEADMAN WONDERLAND
STORY & ART BY JINSEI KATAOKA, KAZUMA KONDOU

DEADMAN WONDERLAND 12

CONTENTS

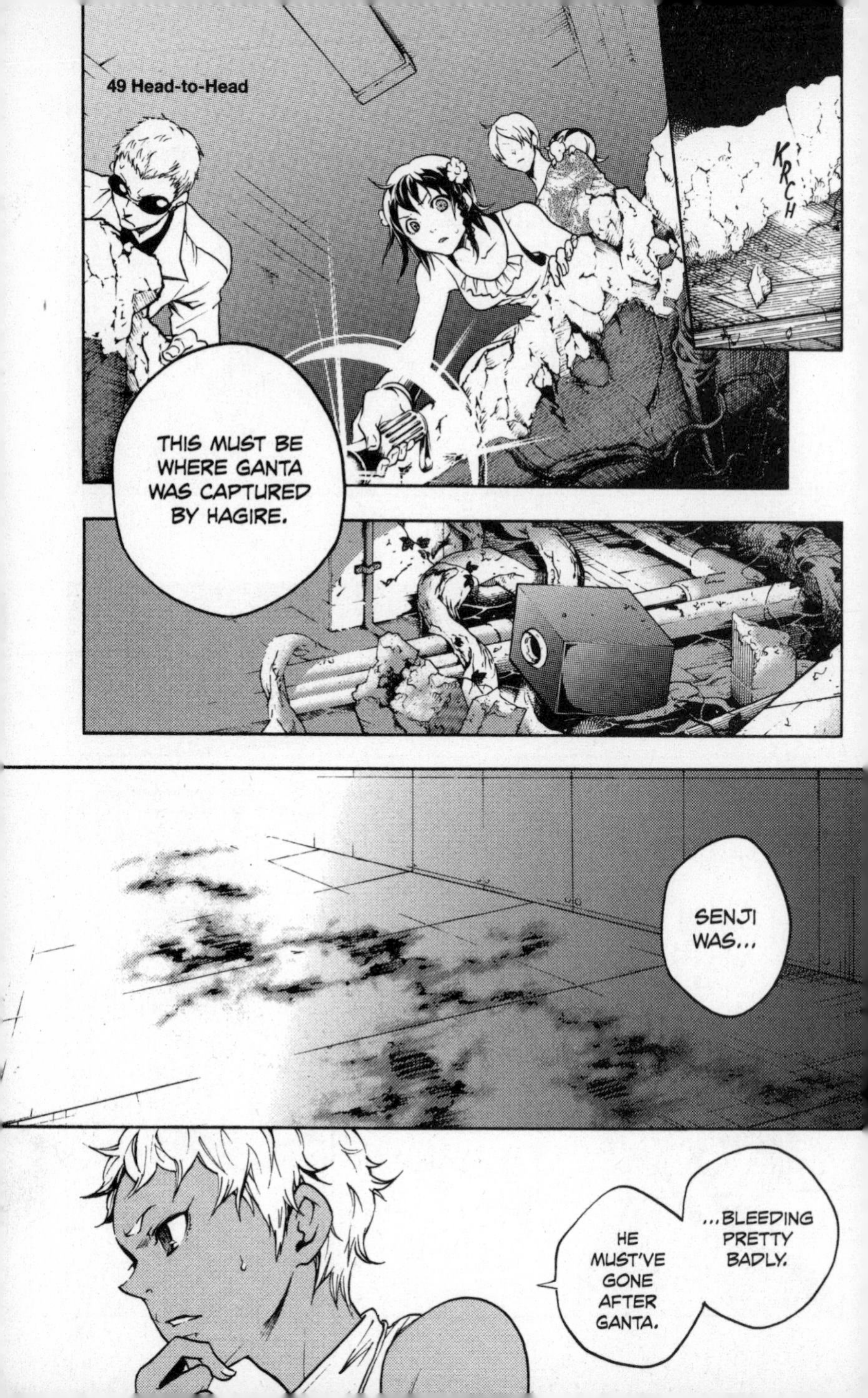
KRCH
THIS MUST BE WHERE GANTA WAS CAPTURED BY HAGIRE.
SENJI WAS...
...BLEEDING PRETTY BADLY.
HE MUST'VE GONE AFTER GANTA.

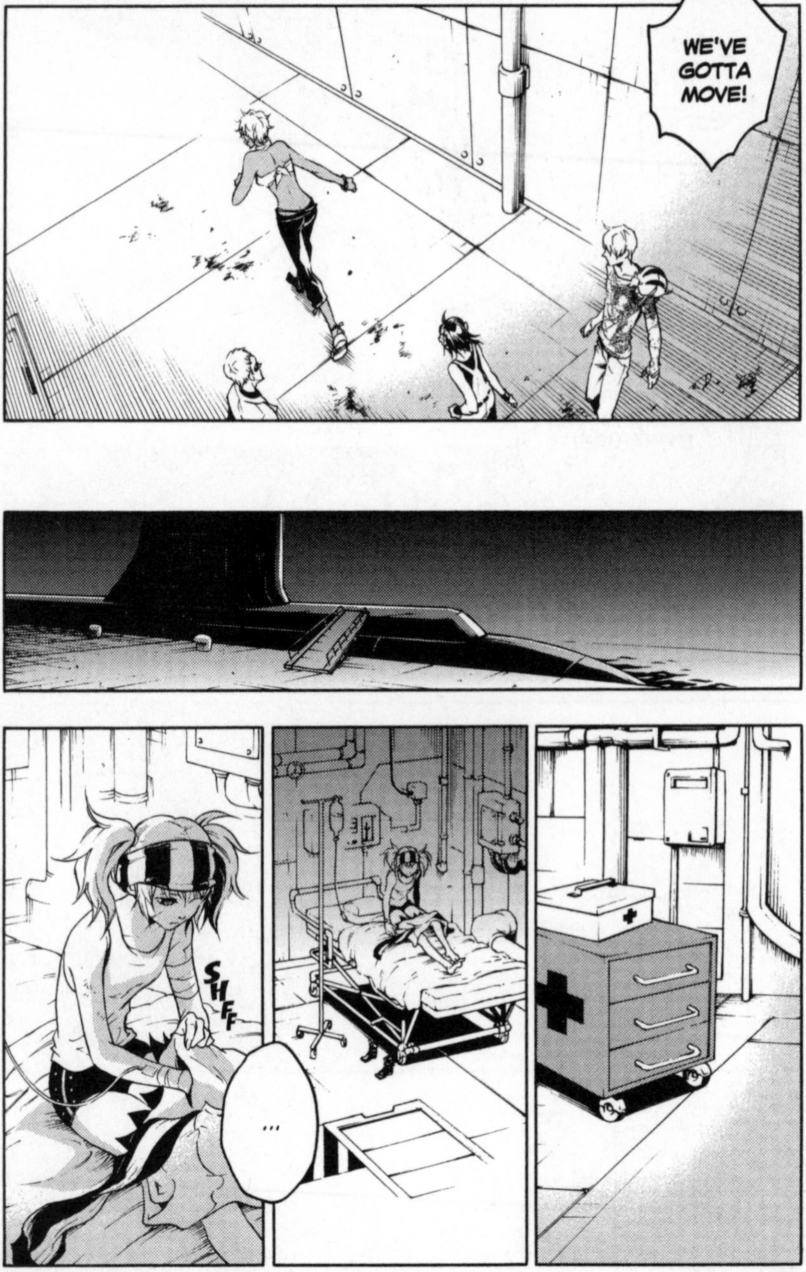
WE'VE GOTTA MOVE!
...
SHFF

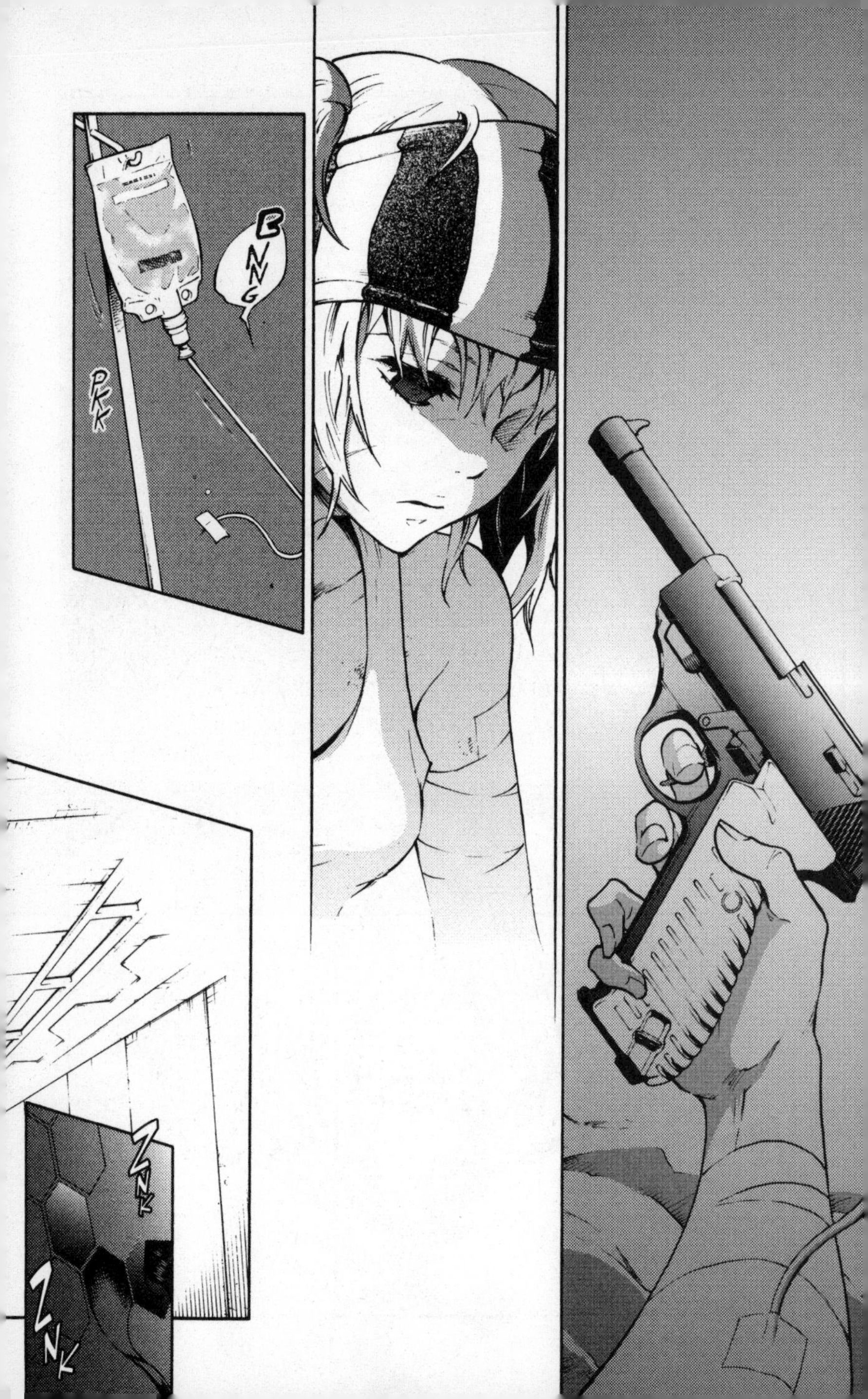
BNNG
PKK
ZNK
ZNK

YOU CAME BACK ON YOUR OWN! WHAT A GOOD BOY. ☆
ZNNK
YEAH... COMPARED TO YOU!
...
THEN LET'S FINISH MY DOWNLOAD. BUT THIS TIME...
CHN
...I'LL CUT YOUR LEGS OFF SO YOU CAN'T GET AWAY.
NYK
DON'T WORRY THOUGH...

WHEN I'M DONE, I'LL PUT THEM BACK ON. ☆
OOO
...!
GANTA!
NO! NO MORE!

NO MORE RUNNING!
SPK
?!
FASTER THAN THE SPEED OF SOUND!
THAT WAS FAST!

SK
FF
AND REMEMBER ...
ZWCH
"IN ACTUAL COMBAT..."
...YOU HAVE TO DO IT IN UNDER HALF A SECOND!
ZWK
ZZK
ZWK
HA!

IT'S THAT BRANCH OF SIN!
?!
URGH!
SLMP
THAT PAIN'S BACK AGAIN!
SWP

HEADS UP.
DOOM

WUSH
KRKK
KRNK
...!
WAS THAT FROM UP-STAIRS ?!
ZWCHH

AH HA! ☆
CH
OK
WRAK
HA HA!
HA HA HA HA!
HA!
KRTAK

SKF...
...!
TOTO!

YANK
TMP TMP
?!
WOO

HFF
SHF
HFF
FWWP
HFF
TEK
YOU CAN STILL MOVE?! WHY AREN'T YOU DEAD?

SHUT UP. WHY ARE YOU STILL ALIVE?
ZSH
ZWP
ZWP
ZWP
SLR
CH
YOUR FOOTWORK IS TERRIBLE.
WHERE ARE YOU EVEN AIMING?
AHA! ☆
KCH...
ZWP

THAT TINY LITTLE KNIGHT YOU'RE COUNTING ON IS IN BAD SHAPE. ☆
ZZWP
...
YOU REALLY DON'T GET IT.
KRK
KRRK

DEADMAN WONDERLAND
OHO!
SO THAT WAS YOUR PLAN!
I CAN HAN-DLE THAT.

HM?
THIS SEEMS ...
NO NAME
... SOMEHOW FAMILIAR.
YEAH.

HE JUST KEEPS ON GETTIN' UP.

KRAK
ZRK
YAAA...
A
ZRK
KRAK
AA
ZRK
KRAK
A

AAAA
AAA

NOT AS MANY TIMES AS YOU DO, CROW.
?!
OF COURSE NOT!

TH- THEY'RE ...
...A TEAM!

NNN
WIK

S-S-
SLICE!

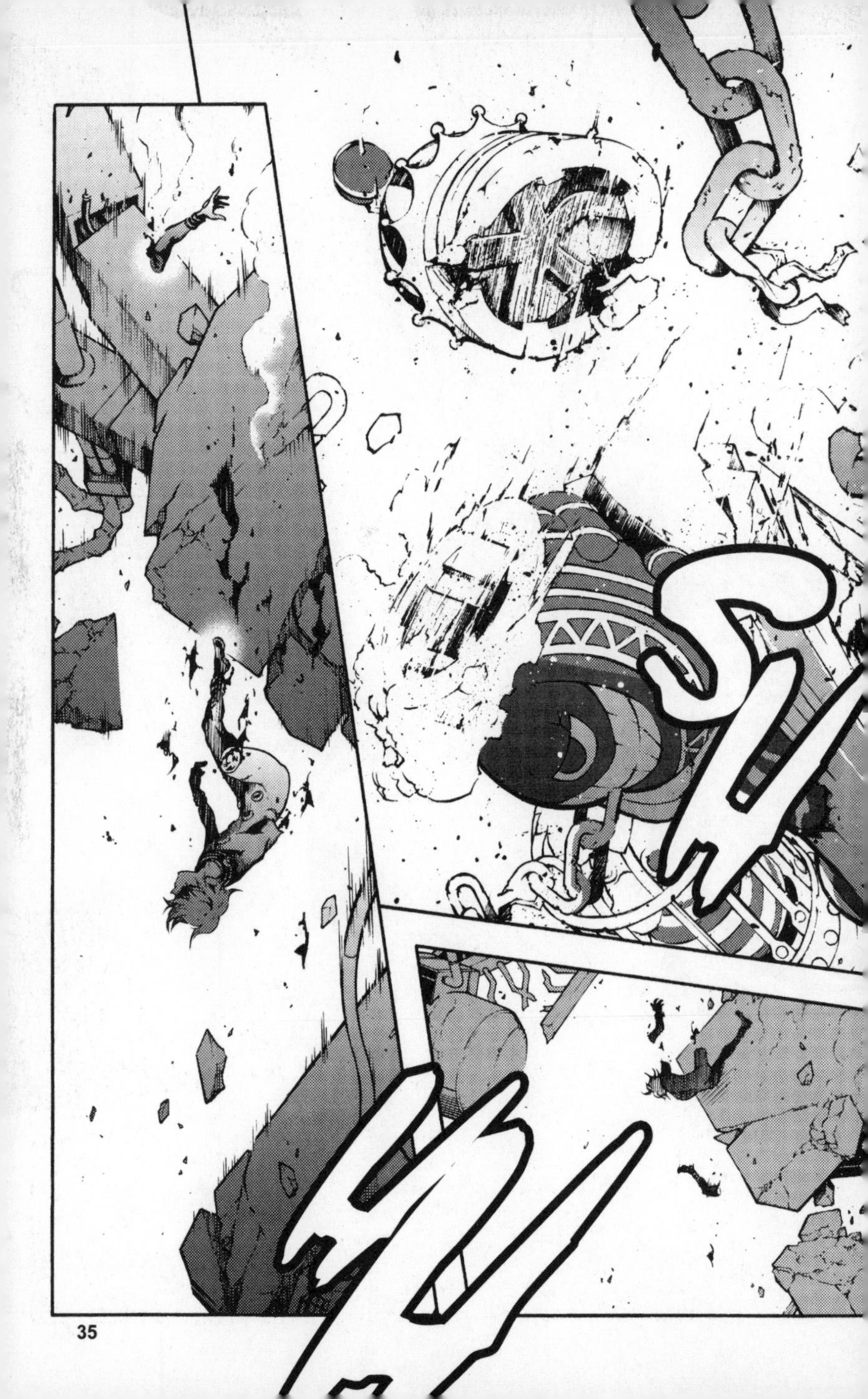

GSHH

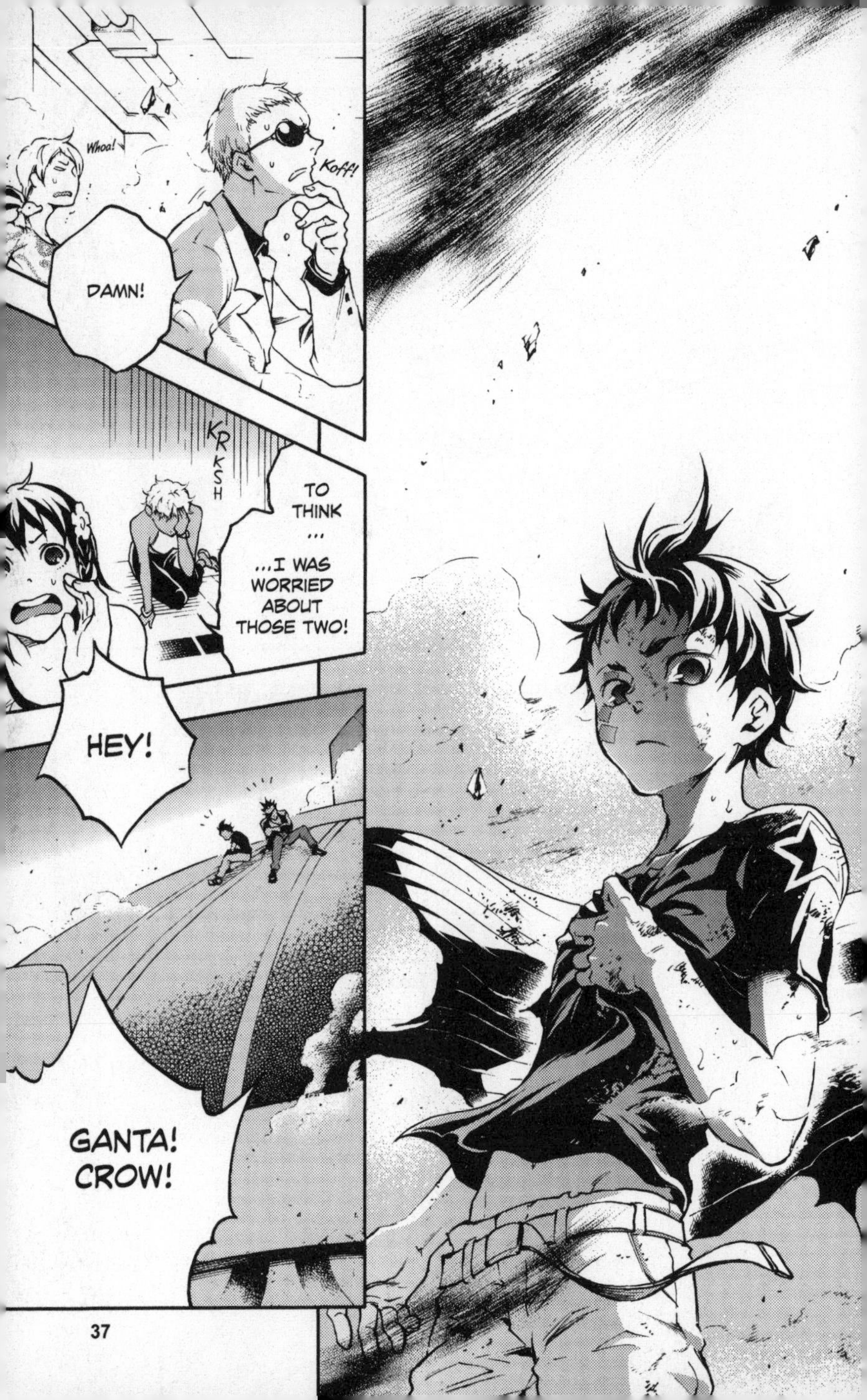
Koff!
Whoa!
DAMN!
KRKSH
TO THINK ...
...I WAS WORRIED ABOUT THOSE TWO!
HEY!
GANTA! CROW!

WAY TO KICK ASS!
BUMP

TK...
TOTO...
YOU DEAD?

BECAUSE
...
...I HAVEN'T PUMPED YOU FULL OF LEAD YET.

DWL

DEADMAN WONDERLAND

DWL

DEADMAN WONDE

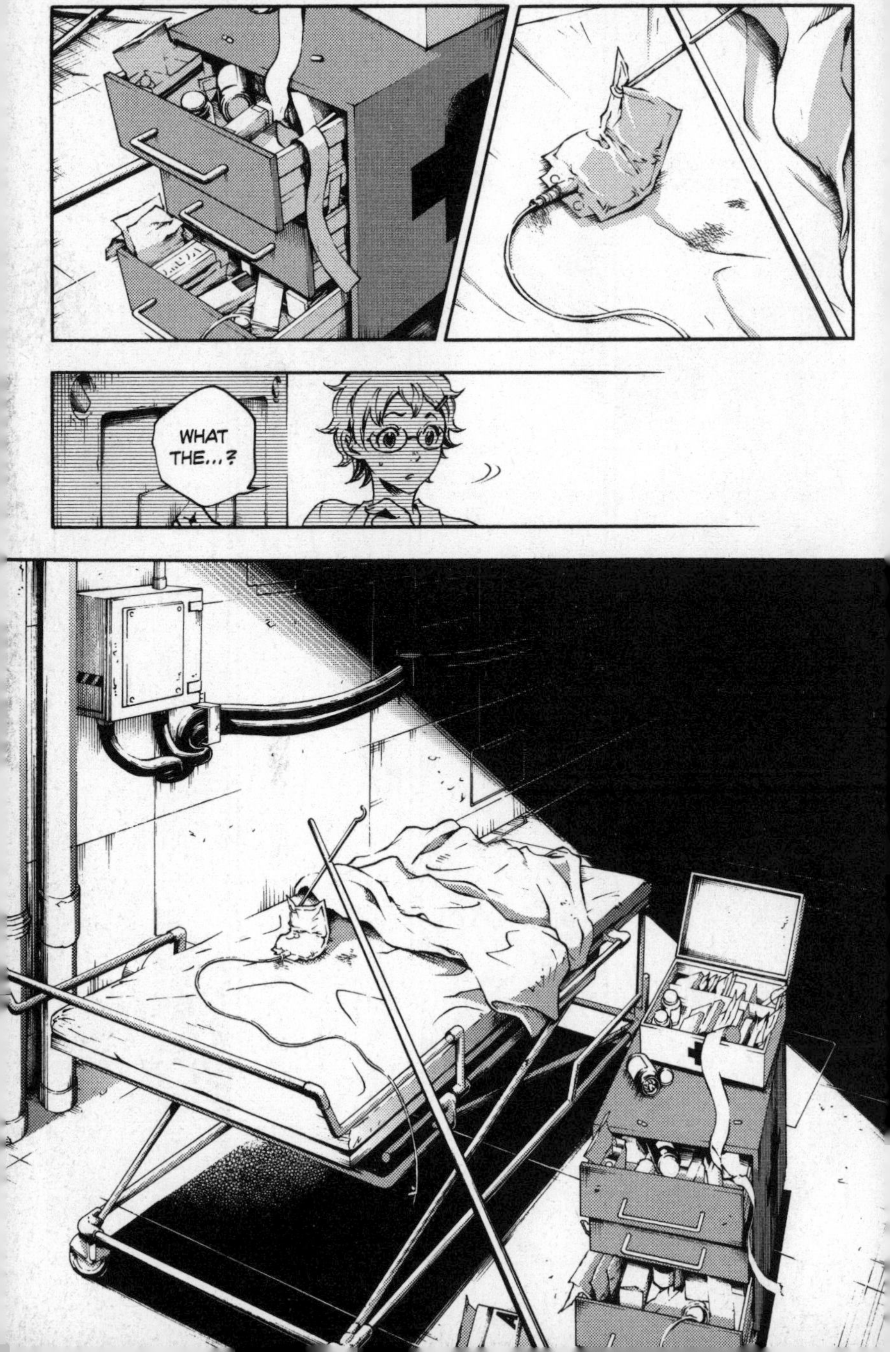
WHAT THE...?

HFF
SKCH
SKCH
SKCH
HFF
HF
HFF
HANG IN THERE...
... TOTO!

I STILL
...
...DON'T KNOW TOTO'S REASON.

SHE'S JUST A SKINNY LITTLE GIRL. I BET SHE'S...
...NOT REALLY EVEN A DEADMAN!
WHAM
JUST FALSELY ACCUSED.
LET'S HAVE SOME FUN BEFORE YOU DIE IN CARNIVAL CORPSE.
SKF
OH!

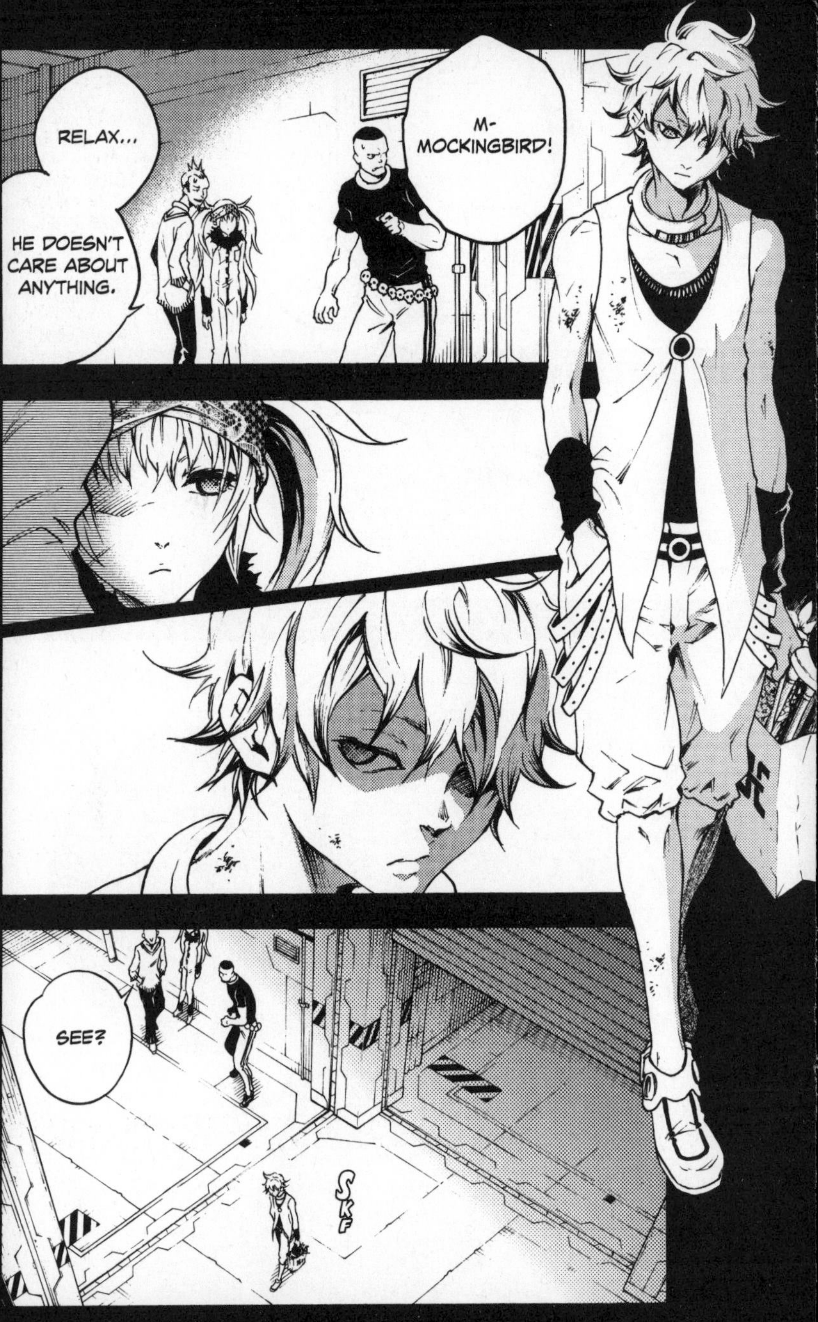
M-MOCKINGBIRD!
RELAX...
HE DOESN'T CARE ABOUT ANYTHING.
SEE?
SKF

THAT WEIRDO IN THE GLASSES SAID G WARD'S SUPER DANGEROUS. YOU CAN DIE HERE AND...
...THAT'S KINDA PERFECT.
I THINK?
?
YOSUGA WANTS TO DIE... KINDA.
I MEAN, I DON'T HAVE MUCH REASON TO LIVE, DO I?

WHOA! ☆
SWEET! SHE'S A NUT-JOB!
SHE'S JUST CREEPING ME OUT.
SISH
I'LL SLIT HER THROAT. YOU CAN STICK IT IN THERE!
YOU ARE ONE SICK...
ZNNK
...BAS-
SPLRCH

YOU'RE MY LONG-LOST BIG SISTER!
H-HUH?

KLTTR
WE NEED MORE BLOOD!
AND DOUBLE THE ANESTHESIA!
WE'LL OPEN HIS THIGH AND SET THE BONE!
I know!
...
...
Operating Room Do Not Enter
GAME FOWL USED TO BE A NURSE, EH?
She's bossing the doctor around.
KINDA WEIRD.
KCHK
THAT GUY'S TOO TOUGH TO QUIT.
HOW...
HOW'S GANTA DOING?

THE WOUNDS DON'T SEEM TO BE THE PROBLEM...
WSH
!

BOOMP
G
HEY, SIS!
SH
I WON AGAIN TODAY!
ING!!
WHY DO YOU COME HERE EVERY DAY?
Stop breaking the lock!
KCH
MY NAME'S TOTO!

YEAH, I GET IT. YOU'RE TO...
...TO!
GULP
UUGH!
KOFF
KOFF
YOU'RE WEAK, SIS, SO I'LL CARE FOR US BOTH.
I DON'T NEED YOUR HELP...
...AND I'M ***NOT*** YOUR BIG SISTER!
HZZ
HZZ
OUR LAST NAMES ARE DIFFERENT.
YOU'RE 18, RIGHT?
I'M ONLY 17!

OH.
I KNOW THAT BOOK.
THE PRIVATE DETECTIVE'S THE KILLER, RIGHT? WHAT'S UP WITH THAT?
SO?
...
CARNIVAL CORPS
ROD
NOOOOOOO
WHAT? I WON?!
WBBL
WHY WON'T THIS DAMN BRANCH OF SIN...

...LET ME DIE?
MAYBE ONCE I LEARN TO CONTROL IT BETTER...
...I CAN MAKE IT LEAVE ME ALONE.
YOSUGA LOST IT ALL THAT DAY.
I HAVE NOTHING LEFT. AND YET THE POLICE...
...CHILD PROTECTIVE SERVICES...
...AND EVEN MY NEW SIBLING...

WHY DO THEY ALL KEEP TRYING TO KEEP ME ALIVE?
DOES ANYBODY HAVE A REASON TO LIVE?

YOU'RE LOOKING FOR MOCKINGBIRD'S WEAKNESS?
KAH HA HA
HE'S ALMOST AS TALENTED AS WRETCHED EGG. YOU NEED ALL THE EDGE YOU CAN GET.
I LIKE HOW YOU THINK.
THAT'S NOT WHAT I'M...
MOCKING-BIRD'S CRAZY...

HE'S POWERFUL, BUT MORE THAN THAT... HE'S SCARY!
CORPSE
AHHH...
RECORDS SAY THERE WAS...
...AN OLDER SISTER, BUT SHE DIED IN THE GREAT EARTHQUAKE. ABOUT THE PARENTS...
...THERE'S NOTHING. AN ORPHAN IT LOOKS LIKE.
VERY MUCH LIKE YOU. IT'S NOT THAT UNCOMMON.
HE KINDA ...

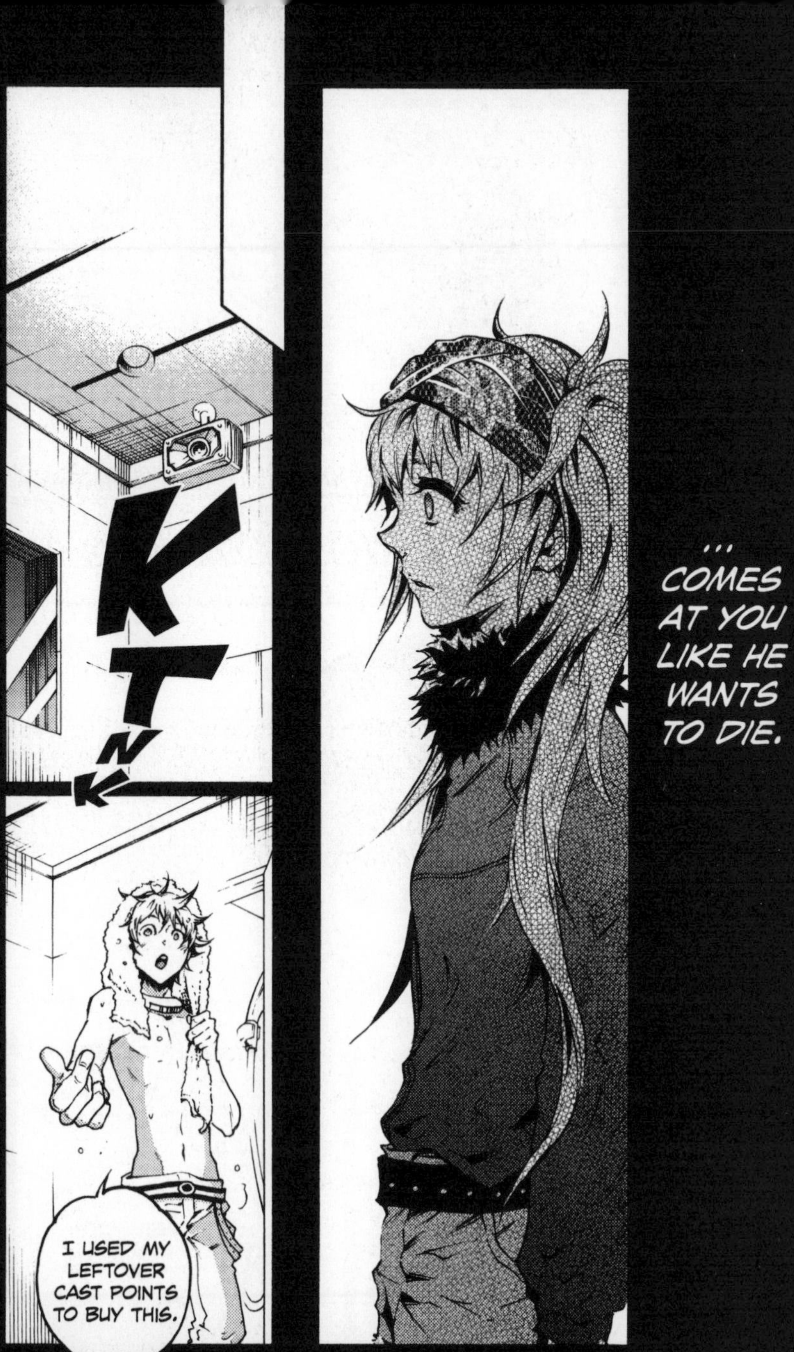
...COMES AT YOU LIKE HE WANTS TO DIE.
KTNK
I USED MY LEFTOVER CAST POINTS TO BUY THIS.

NICE, HUH? IT'S FOR YOU.
BANG!
ONE SHOT ...
...AND YOU CAN DIE ANYTIME YOU WANT!
IS YOSUGA GOING TO FILL YOU WITH LEAD?
YUP. AND I'LL TEAR YOU APART.

SO NO MATTER WHAT HAPPENS... NO MATTER HOW BAD IT GETS...
...I CAN DIE ANY TIME I WANT?
HEH HEH.
YUP. REASSURING, RIGHT?
YEAH... IT IS.
SO FROM NOW ON... THIS IS YOUR REASON TO LIVE!

...
PLIP
WAIT A SECOND. IT'S MADE OF PLASTIC.
YUP.
IT'S A TOY.
HEH HEH.

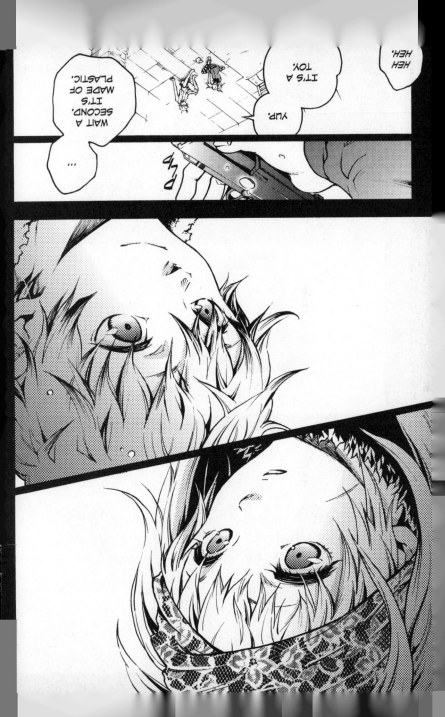

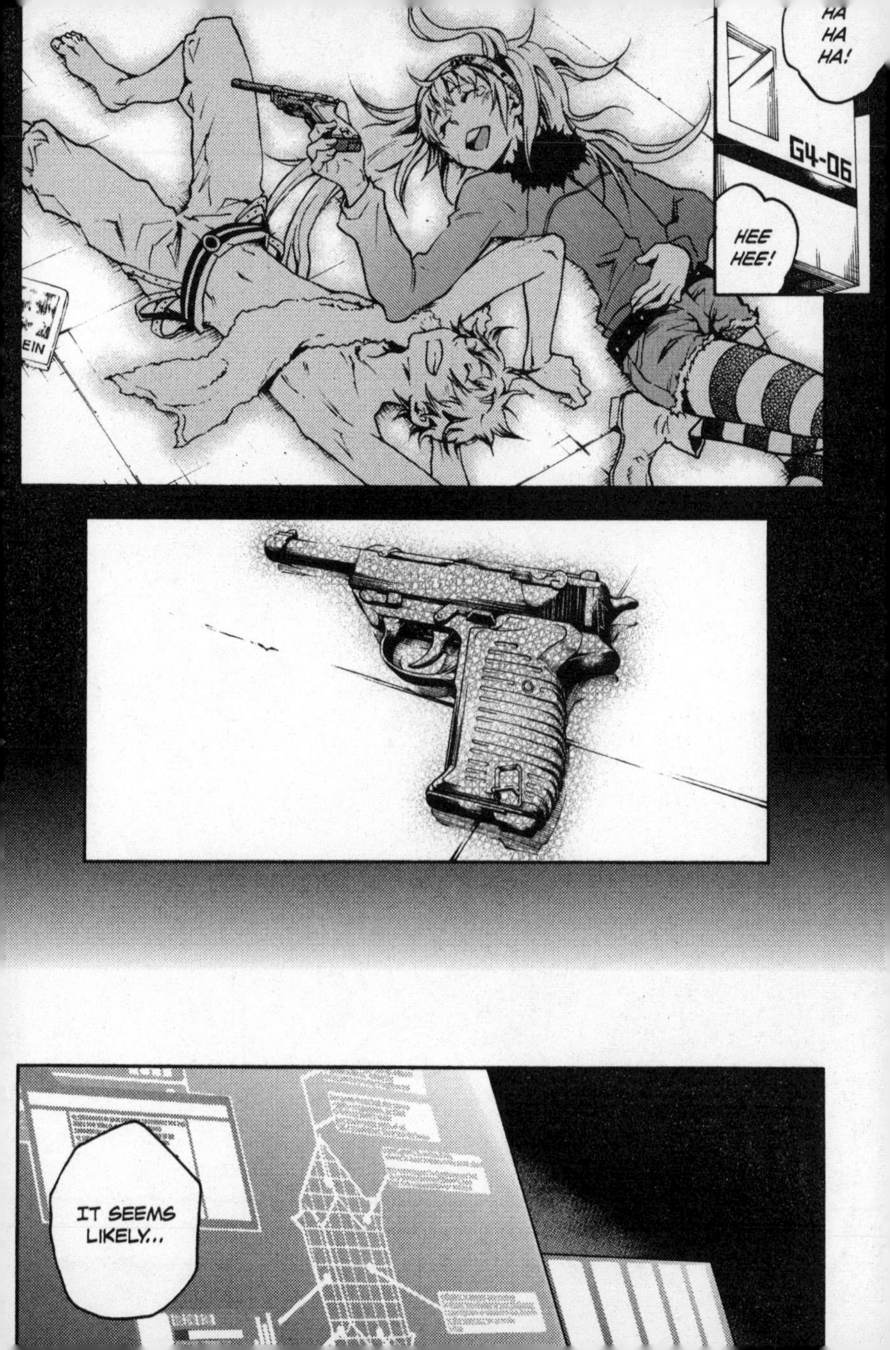
HA HA HA!
G4-06
HEE HEE!
EIN
IT SEEMS LIKELY...

...THAT HE WAS IN CONSTANT PAIN.
THE NAMELESS WORM THAT MAKES UP HIS BRANCH OF SIN IS EATING AWAY AT HIS MUSCLE AND NERVE TISSUES.
IN A VERY REAL SENSE, HE'S OVER-HEATING.
THERE'S NOTHING IN THE FILES DOCUMENTING OTHER CASES LIKE THIS.
IS IT BECAUSE GANTA IGARASHI'S BRANCH OF SIN IS UNIQUE?
I THINK THAT THE MORE...
...HE USES HIS ABILITIES THE WORSE HE'LL...
WHEREVER YOU GO, IT'S THE CHILDREN THAT SUFFER.
EVEN IF GANTA WANTS TO FIGHT HER...
...WE HAVE TO FORTIFY THE MOTHER-GOOSE SYSTEM AND SEAL WRETCHED EGG.

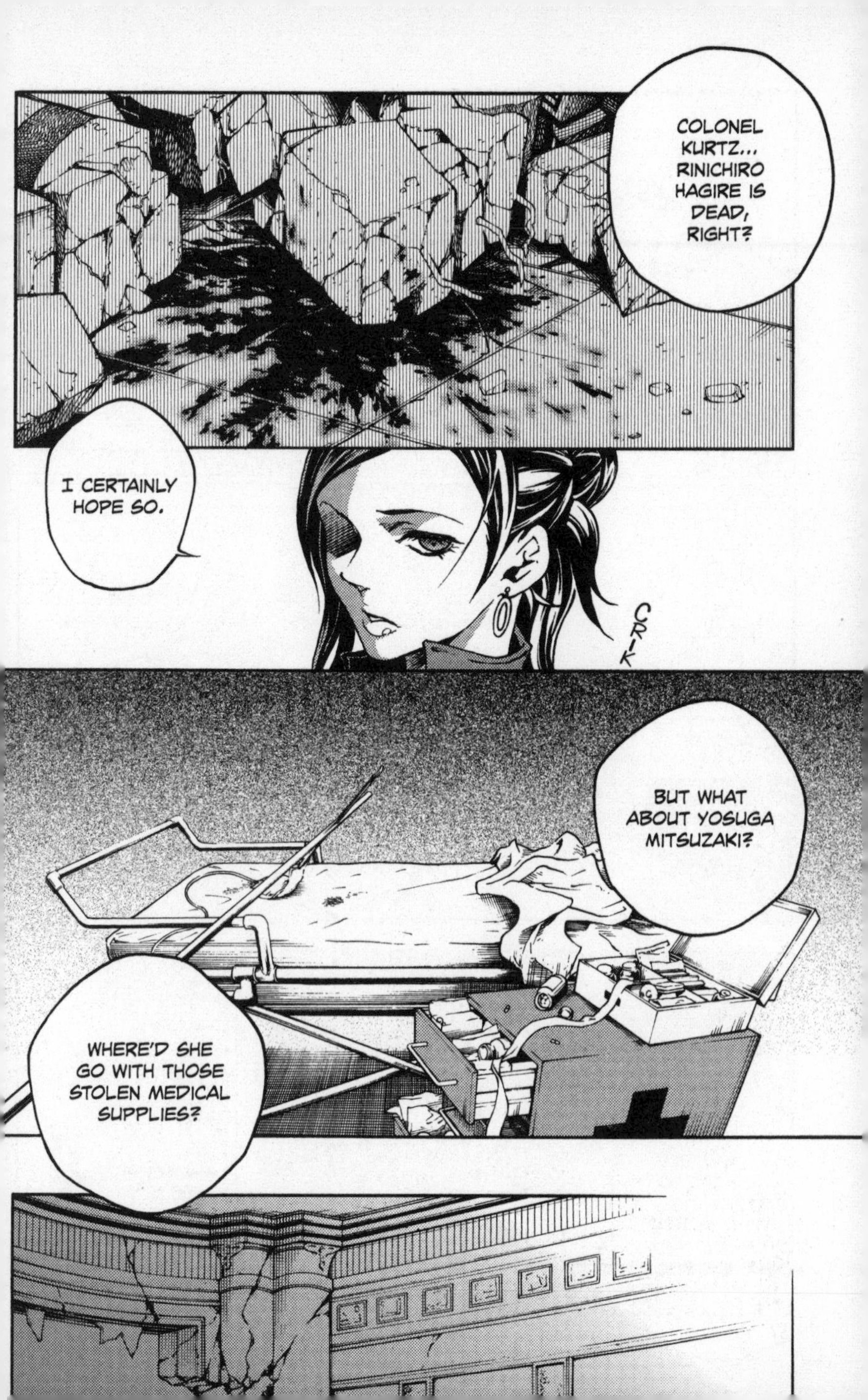
COLONEL KURTZ... RINICHIRO HAGIRE IS DEAD, RIGHT?
I CERTAINLY HOPE SO.
CRIK
BUT WHAT ABOUT YOSUGA MITSUZAKI?
WHERE'D SHE GO WITH THOSE STOLEN MEDICAL SUPPLIES?

...
HUH?
KLNG
SPSH

WH...
WHO...
HZZ
WHO ARE YOU?
HFF
YOSUGA ...
BUT YOU'VE ALWAYS JUST CALLED ME SIS.

DEADMAN WONDERLAND

DW

DE

WONDER

AND

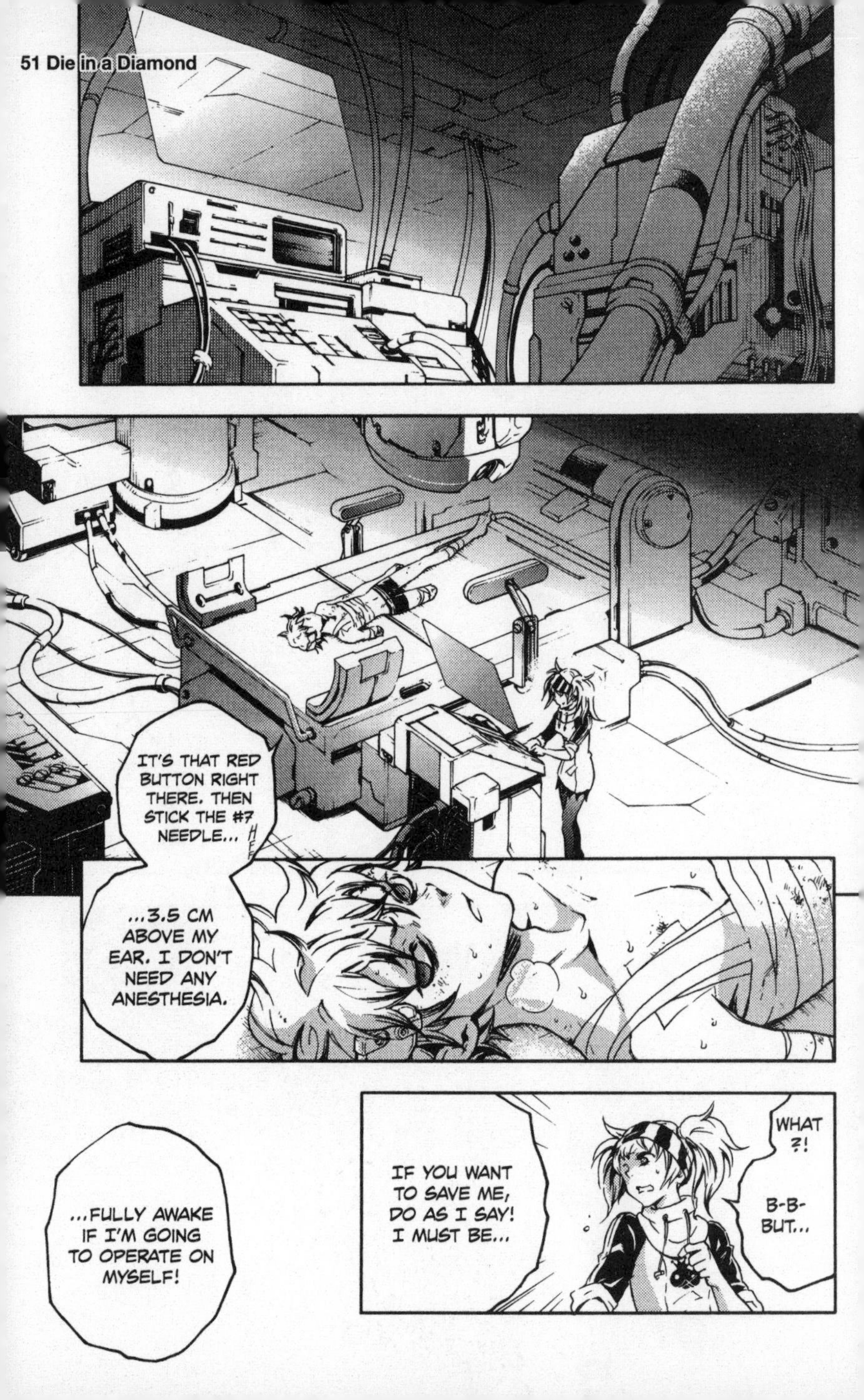
IT'S THAT RED BUTTON RIGHT THERE. THEN STICK THE #7 NEEDLE...
HF
...3.5 CM ABOVE MY EAR. I DON'T NEED ANY ANESTHESIA.
WHAT ?!
B-B-BUT...
IF YOU WANT TO SAVE ME, DO AS I SAY! I MUST BE...
...FULLY AWAKE IF I'M GOING TO OPERATE ON MYSELF!

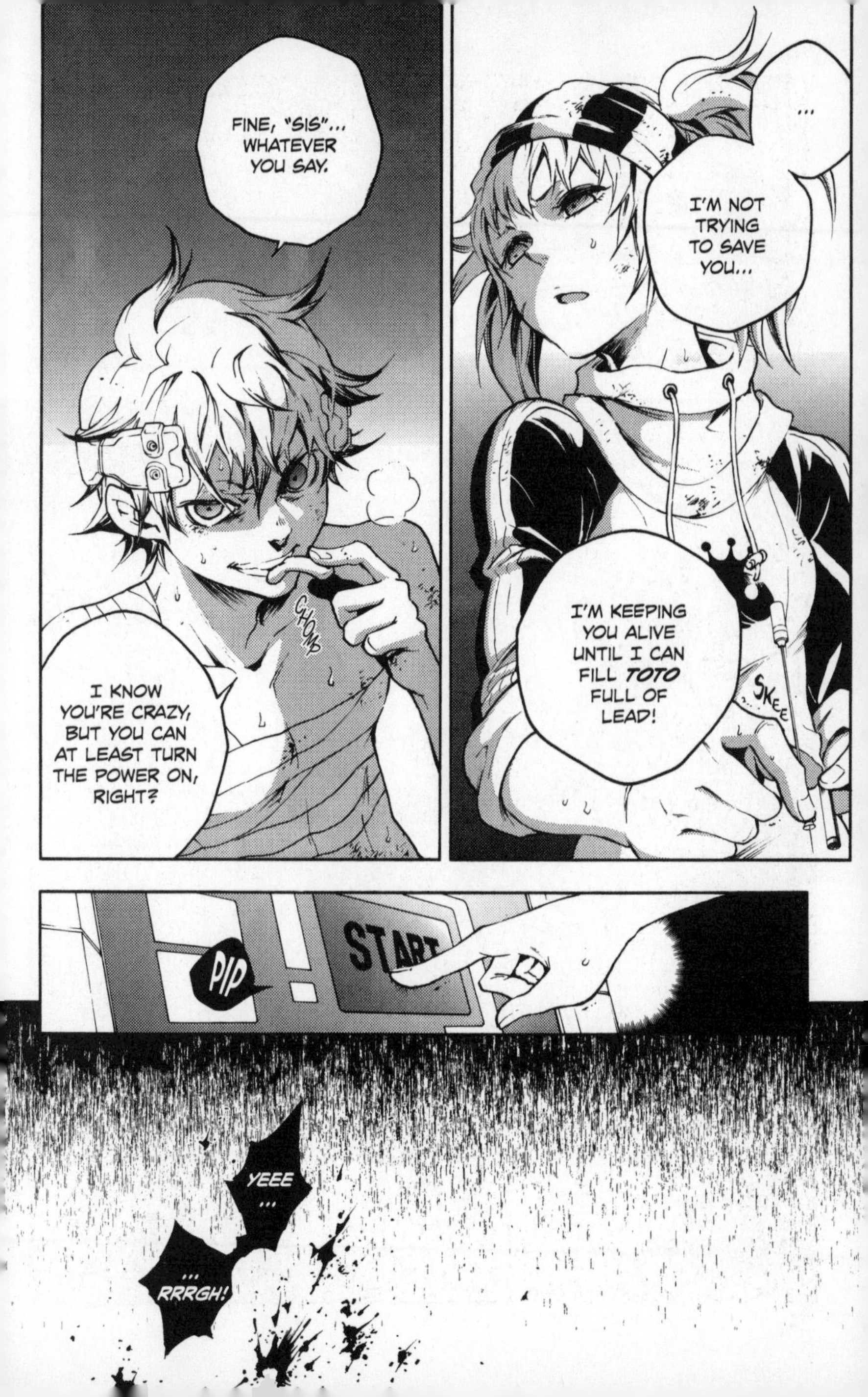
...
I'M NOT TRYING TO SAVE YOU...
I'M KEEPING YOU ALIVE UNTIL I CAN FILL *TOTO* FULL OF LEAD!
SKEE
FINE, "SIS"... WHATEVER YOU SAY.
CHOMP
I KNOW YOU'RE CRAZY, BUT YOU CAN AT LEAST TURN THE POWER ON, RIGHT?
START
PIP
YEEE...
...RRRGH!

51 Die in a Diamond

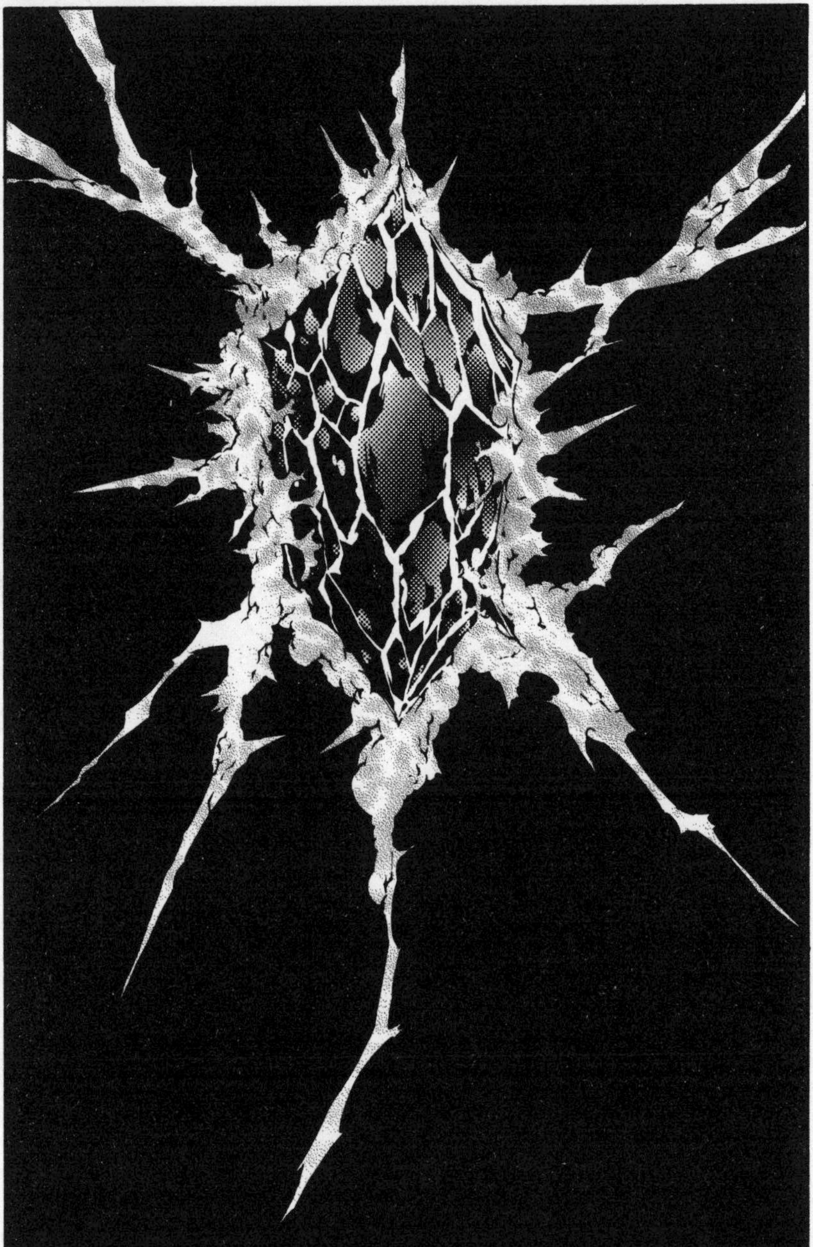

SORRY I'M LATE!
B
A
M
HOW LONG WAS I ASLEEP?!
GOOD MORNING! GLAD YOU'RE UP!
WE WERE STARTING TO WORRY ABOUT YOU.
Uh...
YOU WERE ASLEEP FOR ABOUT FIVE MEALS.
What?!
THAT LONG?!
DUDE.
YOU SHOULDA STAYED IN BED.
SKF
THAT WAY I'D GET TO EAT YOUR SHARE.
CROW!

YO.
...
OH!
WHAT?
I'M FINE AS LONG I TAKE MY PAIN MEDS.
WOULD'VE BEEN A LOT WORSE IF NOT FOR YOU.
PRETTY COOL, HUH? KINDA LIKE TANGE SAZEN!
I love those movies!
Tange...?
...
IT REALLY IS YOU.

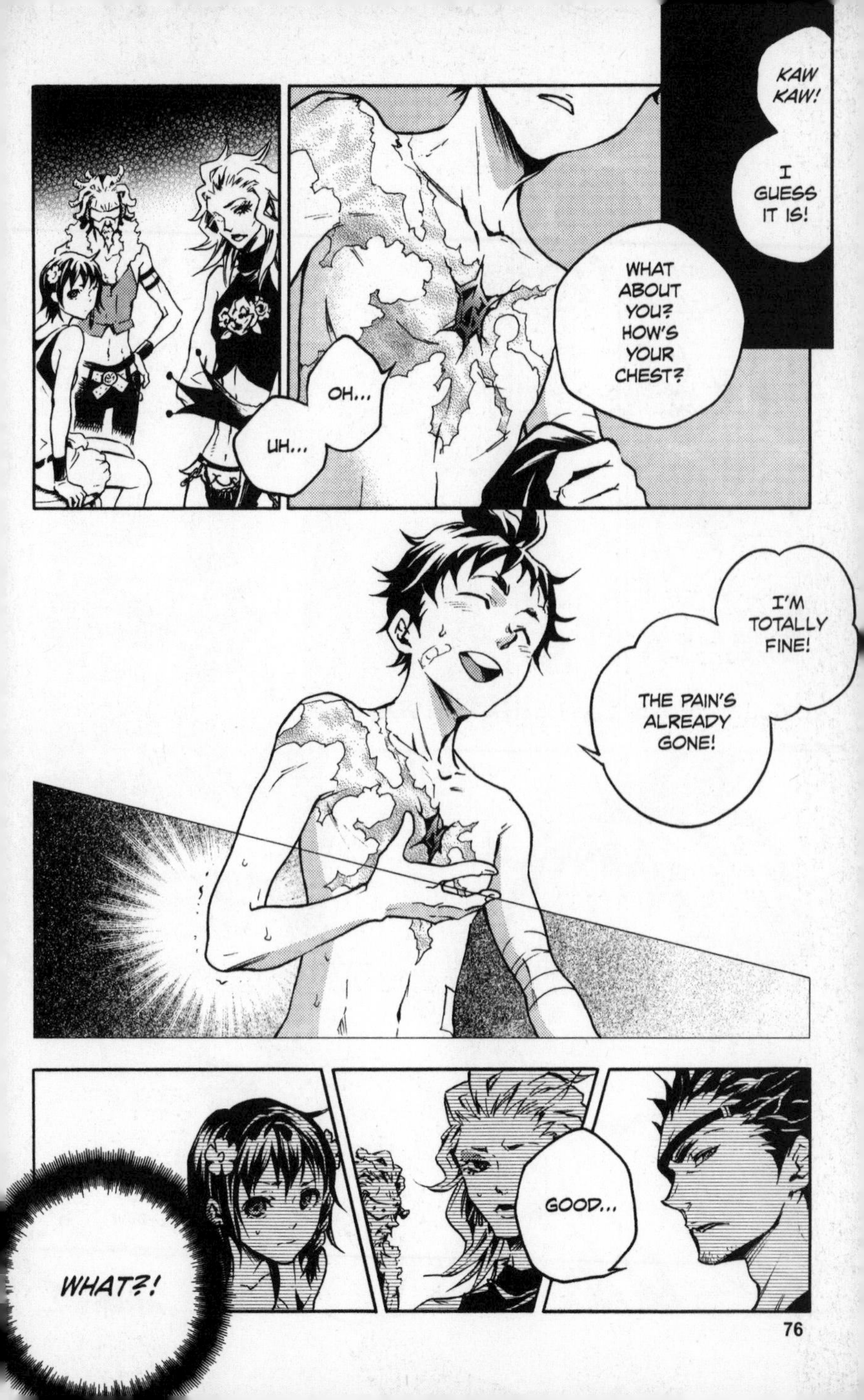
KAW KAW!
I GUESS IT IS!
WHAT ABOUT YOU? HOW'S YOUR CHEST?
OH...
UH...
I'M TOTALLY FINE!
THE PAIN'S ALREADY GONE!
GOOD...
WHAT?!

WHADDYA MEAN GANTA CAN'T BE HEALED?!
IGARASHI'S BRANCH OF SIN IS TOO UNIQUE.
HIS BRANCH OF SIN... BASICALLY THE VOLUNTARY BLOOD IS EATING AWAY AT HIS INVOLUNTARY MUSCLES.
INVOL-WHAT?
THINGS LIKE INTERNAL ORGANS THAT YOU CAN'T MOVE ON YOUR OWN.
HE MOST LIKELY WON'T BE ABLE TO SUSTAIN HIS BODILY FUNCTIONS.
BECAUSE NO HUMAN CAN CONTROL THE BLOOD THAT FLOWS TO THE HEART OR BRAIN...
...IF HE CONTINUES USING HIS BRANCH OF SIN...

...EVENTUALLY HE'LL...
OH, YEAH.
WHERE'S MS. MAKINA?
UH...
SHE WAS IN THE OTHER ROOM.
WHY?
I HAVE SOMETHING KINDA IMPORTANT ...
...I WANT TO TELL HER AND THE OTHERS.
SPISH

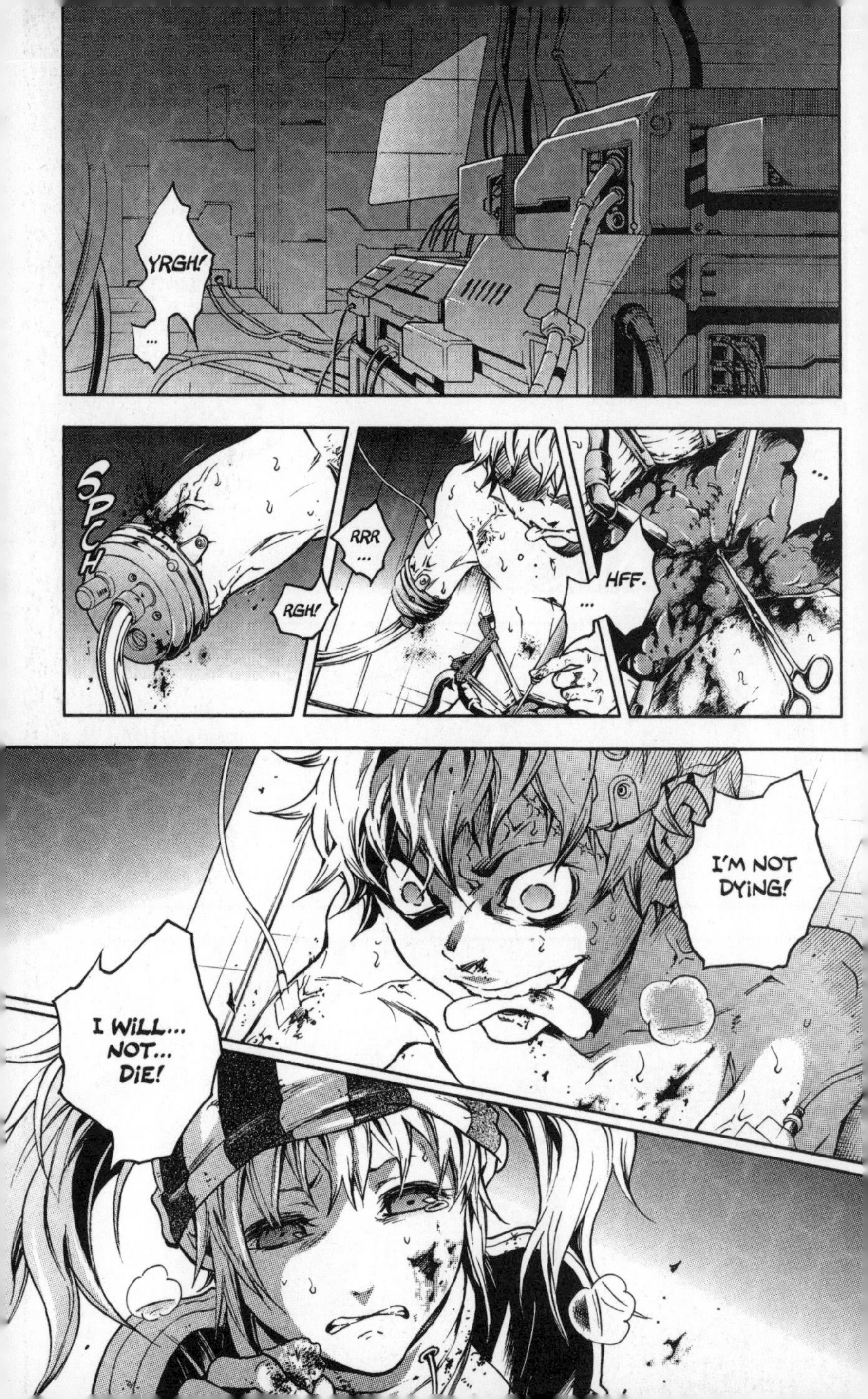

YRGH!
...
...
HFF.
...
RRR
...
RGH!
SPCH
I'M NOT
DYING!
I WILL...
NOT...
DIE!

I'M GOING TO LIVE... FOR HER!
YOU SAW RINICHIRO HAGIRE'S MEMORIES?!
YES.
WHILE WE WERE CONNECTED...
...I SAW ALL KINDS OF THINGS!

INCLUDING HOW TO OPERATE THE MOTHER-GOOSE SYSTEM.
I DON'T KNOW THE SPECIFICS BECAUSE IT'S SOMETHING MOM MADE.
BUT IF YOU USE A PARTICULAR BRANCH OF SIN TO CONNECT THE CIRCUITS...
...I THINK IT CAN UNSEAL OR EVEN STRENGTHEN WRETCHED EGG.
...!
WHOA!
I'M THE KEY.

ALL I HAVE TO DO IS BLAST IT WITH MY MOST POWERFUL BRANCH OF SIN.

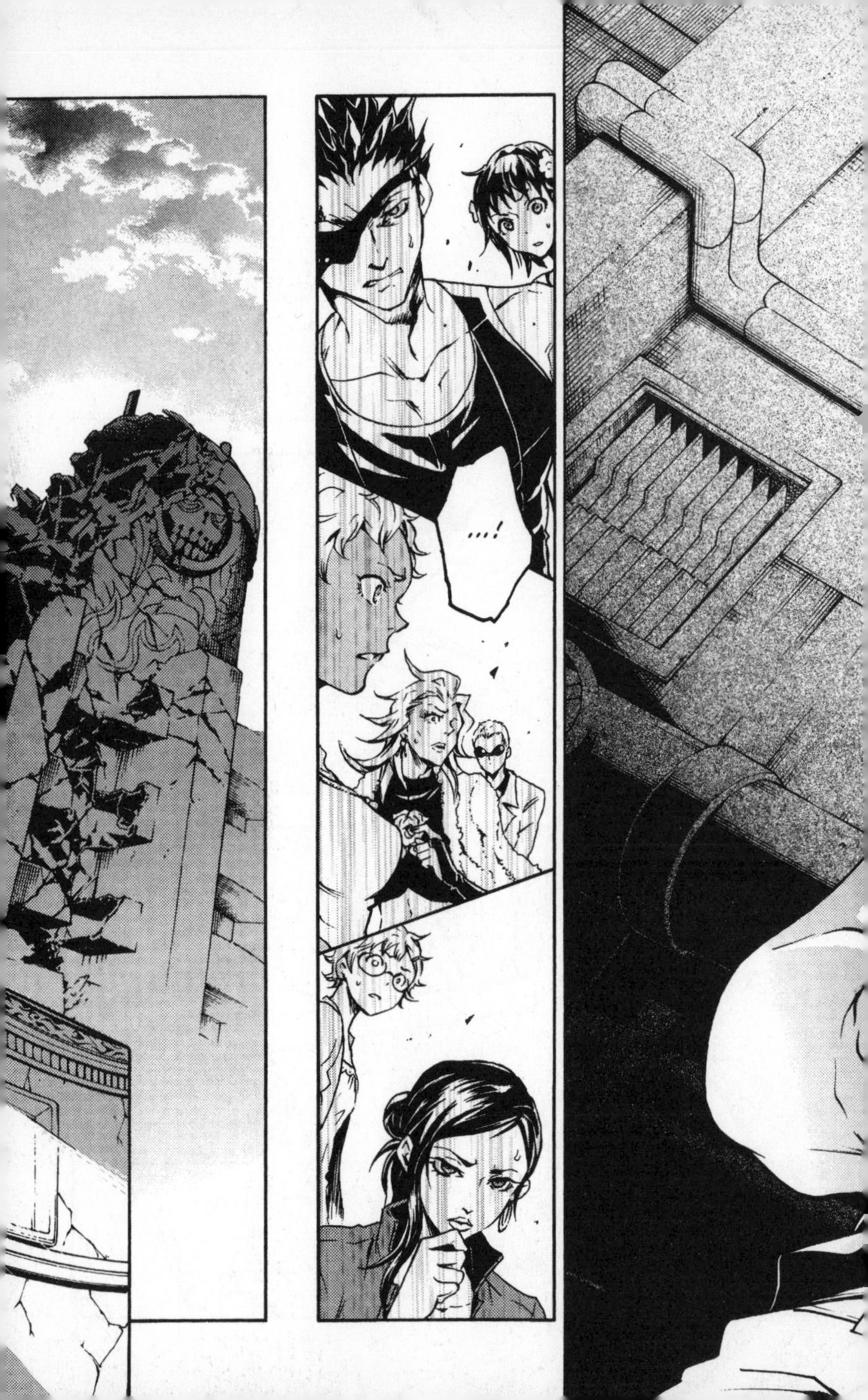

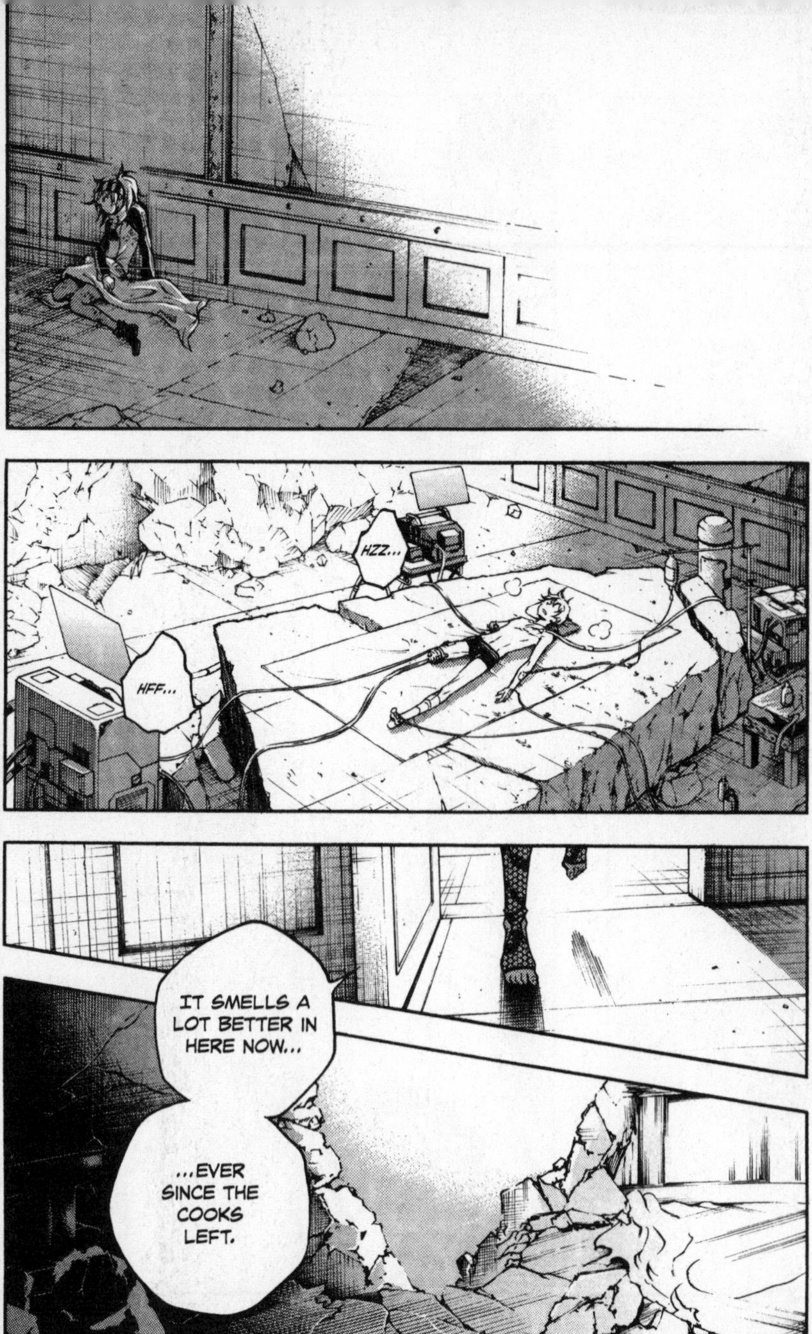
HZZ...
HFF...
IT SMELLS A LOT BETTER IN HERE NOW...
...EVER SINCE THE COOKS LEFT.

ENOUGH WITH THE JOKES...
...SHIRO!
I'M ONLY IN THIS MISERABLE CONDITION BECAUSE I LOVE YOU SO MUCH...
THAT'S WHY...
...I'M LOOKING FOR A PERFECT BODY.
ONE THAT WON'T DIE FROM BEING KILLED!

I WANT THE ULTIMATE YOU AND THE ULTIMATE ME... SO WE CAN LOVE AND KILL ONE ANOTHER!
SO...
KCH
I WILL...

...SET YOU FREE!
...STOP SHIRO ONCE AND FOR ALL!

KRIK
I CAN'T WAIT TO SEE...
...WHICH ONE OF YOU WILL MAKE MY WISH COME TRUE!

LAND DEADMAN WONDERL

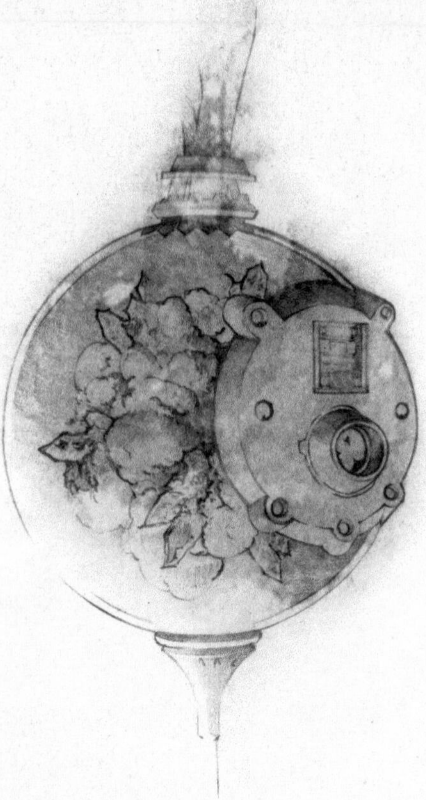

WHAT'S THE MOST ABSURD THING? IT'S GOTTA BE HUMANS!

I PUT THEM IN CAGES AND GAZE AT THEM.

TMP
BEEP
Well?
WE'RE IN.
PIP
I'LL PUT IT UP ON SCREEN.
THAT'S ...

...THE MOTHER-GOOSE SYSTEM?!
THE ACTIVITY CONTROL DEVICE OF WRETCHED EGG'S NAMELESS WORM.
GANTA'S ABILITY IS TO ACT AS THE SYSTEM'S KEY...
...ALLOWING HIM TO EITHER STRENGTHEN OR REMOVE THE SEAL.
? ? ?
THAT'S RIGHT.

SHE CAUSED THE GREAT TOKYO EARTH-QUAKE...
POTENTIALLY, SHE COULD CAUSE EVEN GREATER DESTRUCTION. SO TO STOP HER...
...THEY BUILT THIS-HER FIRST AND FINAL CAGE!
ZING

TP
SHIRO...
BIP BIP
CHK
WHAT WOULD YOU WANT ME TO DO?
TP
FSHH
IT'S OKAY FOR ME TO USE THE POWER YOU GAVE ME...
...TO STOP YOU ONCE AND FOR ALL... ISN'T IT?

...
URGH ...
ZZK
ARGH ...
ZZK
AARGH!
AAR ...
... RGH!
ZZZ
AARGH!
ZZK
KLIK
...!
THE DEVICE IS EMITTING THE SAME ELECTRO-MAGNETIC WAVE...
...THAT A PERSON WOULD! THE CODE IS BEING REWRITTEN!
PIP
UNLOCK
UNLOCK
BEEP UNLOCK
LOCK
PIP

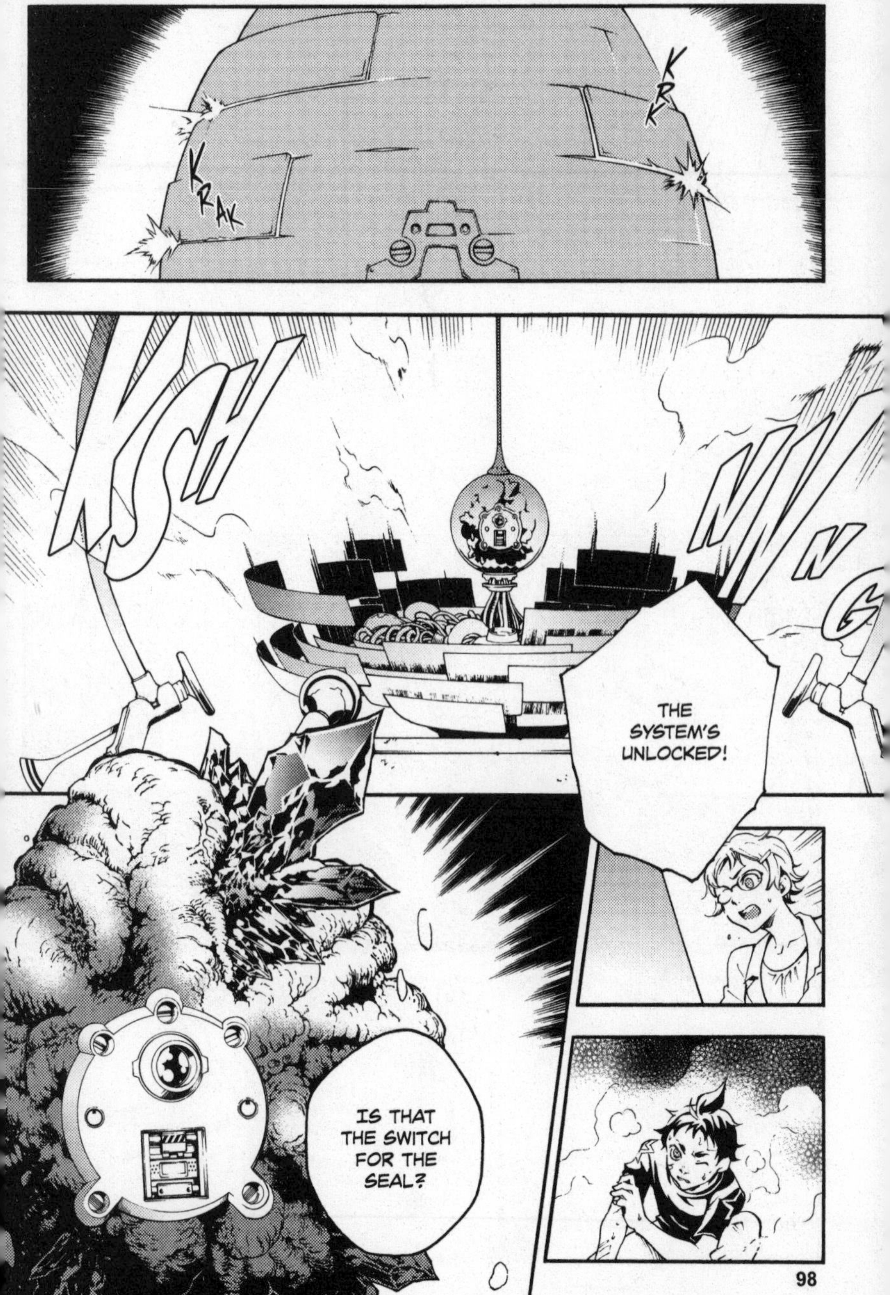
KRK
KRAK
KSH
NNNG
THE SYSTEM'S UNLOCKED!
IS THAT THE SWITCH FOR THE SEAL?

IS IT ALSO MADE FROM WRETCHED EGG'S BODY TISSUE?!
WHAT AWFUL TECHNOL-OGY!
SHWR
YEAH...
OKAY, GANTA IGARASHI ...
...IT'S ALL UP TO YOU NOW.
BECAUSE YOU'RE THE ONLY ONE...
...WHO CAN PUT AN END TO THIS HIDEOUS PAST.
Diary
2002.1
Sorae · Igarashi
HFF
HF
ZNNG
DAMN IT!
IT FEELS LIKE MY VEINS ARE ON FIRE.
ZNNG...
YOU ALL RIGHT, GANTA?
OH... YEAH.

ALL THAT'S LEFT IS TO FLIP THAT SWITCH...
KABOOM
?!
AHA! ☆

SO *THAT'S* WRETCHED EGG'S ACTIVITY CONTROL!
THANKS FOR OPENING IT.
I CAN'T EVEN BEGIN TO TELL YOU THE TROUBLE I WENT THROUGH TRYING TO UNLOCK THAT SWITCH!
RINICHIRO ...
... HAGIRE ...
IS THAT YOU?

THAT BASTARD'S STILL...?!
WHAT?
HE'S JUST AN OLD GEEZER WHO'S BARELY ALIVE...

FOR NOW!
ZOK
ZOK
HE BLOCKED IT?!
I'M SORRY, BUT...

...I CAN'T JUST LET YOU KILL TOTO.
ALL YOSUGA KNOWS IS HOW TO PROVIDE PROTECTION...
...AND TOTO IS THE ONLY ONE THAT I'LL PROTECT.
HMPH ...
DO WHAT YOU WANT, FOOL.
KCH
SLRCH
NOW...

FWP
GET OUT OF MY WAY, YOU GNATS!

ZWT
ZWSH
ZWT
ZWT
ZWT
ZWT
KOFF ...
YOU ...
... GOTTA BE KIDDIN' ME!
HE STILL HAS *THAT* KINDA POWER?!
SKRF
HA!

I WILL MOVE HEAVEN AND EARTH TO FREE HER! TO KILL HER AND TO LOVE HER!
SHE MUST ONCE AGAIN DIG DEEP THAT WONDERFUL HOLE OF ABSURDITY!
SHE MUST DESTROY ALL THE LIES!

LIKE SHE DID TEN YEARS AGO!

SHE MUST EXPOSE ALL THE ABSURDITIES!

HOSPITAL

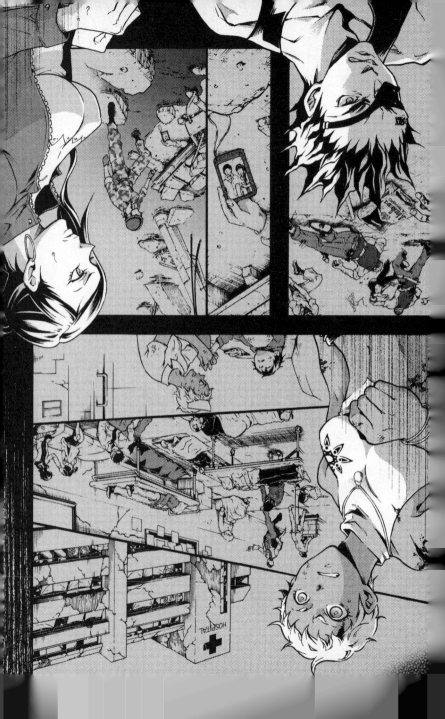

SUPPLIES
UGH!

SCREW THAT!
WE AIN'T GONNA LET THAT HAPPEN!
TMMP
I'M NOT GOING TO GO THROUGH THAT...
...SEE THAT DREADFUL SIGHT...
...LIVE THROUGH THAT AWFUL SADNESS EVER AGAIN!

WE DON'T NEED ANY MORE ABSURDITY!
I DIDN'T CREATE THE ABSURDITIES...
SPLRCH
IT WAS PEOPLE LIKE YOU!
RCH

CH
RO
IT WAS CHIRPING BIRDS LIKE YOU THAT COULDN'T ACCEPT ABSURDITY...
...AND THAT CREATED A MINIATURE GARDEN THAT THE WORLD CALLED...
...DEADMAN WONDERLAND! GROVEL IN FEAR AT THE ECHO OF YOUR SINS!

CLAP
I HAVE ZERO INTEREST...
...IN FOOLS SUCH AS YOU. ☆
URGH ...

KT K
SHF
GRAB
S-
STOP
...
YOU
...
...WILL
NOT LAY
A HAND
ON SHIRO
EVER
AGAIN!

OUT OF MY WAY!
OR I'LL CUT OFF YOUR HEAD...
...LIKE I DID THAT REDHEAD.
HUH?!
YOU KILLED AZAMI?!
DIDN'T YOU KNOW?
THERE'S SOMETHING *ELSE* YOU DON'T KNOW EITHER.
KHF
YOUR MOTHER DESPERATELY TRIED TO HIDE IT FROM YOU.
KCH
I WONDER WHY? IT'S SUCH A BEAUTIFUL TALE.
PERHAPS THERE'S A REASON WHY YOU'RE THE KEY.
BECAUSE "SHIRO"...

W-
WHAT?
SLFF
HA...
HA HA HAHA HA HA!
FEEL THE TRUNK AND THE ROOT OF BRANCH OF SIN!
ZZCH
SIP ITS SWEET NECTAR!

BECAUSE THAT IS YOUR SIN ...
ZZZIK
SLSH
CHK
!
KZZ
KZZK
HEY! STOP MESSIN' AROUND WITH THE KID.

WE HAVEN'T FINISHED OUR DANCE YET!
BD
NN
HAVEN'T YOU HAD ENOUGH?
YOU'RE SCUM BORN FROM THE ASHES OF THE GREAT QUAKE.
TSK
KRK
SO IRRITATING ...
IT'S THOSE EYES... THAT I DESPISE ...
...THE MOST.

WHY ARE YOU LOOKING AT ME LIKE THAT?
LET ME EXPLAIN WHAT I'M ABOUT TO DO.
SINCE YOU ARE SOMEONE STRONG ENOUGH TO WIN CARNIVAL CORPSE...
...I AM TAKING YOUR BODY.
WHAT?! SCREW THAT!
I THOUGHT I WAS GONNA FIGHT WRETCHED EGG!
YOU WILL.
BUT I WILL BE FIGHTING *AS* YOU.
IT'S BEAT UP, BUT THIS BODY WAS THE LAST CHAMPION.
SADLY, THAT MEANS THAT *YOU* HAVE TO DIE.

SO DON'T LOOK AT ME DEFIANTLY. LOOK AT ME...
...WITH FEAR AND DESPERATION. WITH A PLEA FOR YOUR LIFE.
THERE HAVE ALWAYS BEEN TEST SUBJECTS WITH EYES LIKE YOURS.
EYES THAT IRRITATE ME.
WHAT HOPE DOES A PUPPET HAVE WHEN HIS STRINGS ARE CUT?
WHAT ARE YOU SEEING?
I AIN'T DYIN'...
NO WAY!
ZLOOO
I GOT SOMEONE TO LIVE FOR!

I GOT ...
QUIET!
YOU...
YOU...
ZWRRL
WEE
LOVE ☆ LABYRINTH.

NNGH
...
SCATTER!

CHNG
ZOK
...!
SHE'S TROUBLE!
BWIZZG
AAGH!

!
WHAM
KRAK
GRRR...
ZLRCH
OUTTA MY WAY!

OUTTA MY WAY!
OUTTA MY WAY!
SHE AND I ARE GOING TO BE TOGETHER AT LAST!
GET OUT OF MY SIGHT!
GAH!

YOU DECREPIT, PERVERTED OLD MAN!
STOP BABBLING THAT SICK DREAM!
JUST SHUT THE HELL UP AND DIE ALREADY!
KA
BOO
YOU LITTLE INSECTS CANNOT REVERSE THE FLOW OF ABSURDITY...
HACK

USELESS ...
POWER-LESS ...
SHIFT-LESS ...
WORTH-LESS ...
HEARTLESS ...
FUTILE ...
MEANING-LESS...
HACK

IT'S ALL POINTLESS!
AAAH

FWISH!
FWISH!
FWISH!
FWISH!
FWISH!
HZZ...
HZZ...
...!

KRCH
I DON'T KNOW WHAT IT ALL MEANS...
NNGH
WE DEFINITELY LIVE WITH THE ABSURDITY...
CHNG
WE KNOW OUR SINS...
SWFF
BUT...
IT'S *BECAUSE* WE'RE WEAK...

BECAUSE WE'RE POWERLESS ...
SKFF
...THAT WE KEEP ON FIGHTING.
SHFF

SILENCE!
YOU...
YOU...
...DEADMEN!

DEADMAN WONDERLAND

DEADMAN WONDERLAND
DEADMAN WONDERLAND

DEADMAN WONDERLAND

Extra 1-6

DEADMAN WONDERLAND
Extra 1

SSF
SSF
NOM
NOM
IT'S BECAUSE OF YOU, SHIRO!
YIKES
HEY!

BURP
IF I SELL IT, I COULD MAKE 100,000 CPS, BUT...
CHNG
CHNG
...I'LL GET MORE IN THE LONG RUN IF I DO HIM A FAVOR.
SNATCH
CANDY! ♡

CHOMP
MMM! THANKS!
HEY! SHIRO?!
MY CP...
I MEAN, MY MONEY TREE!
I MEAN, MY CANDY!
...
PTEW

EWW! THAT TASTED BAD!
WAAAH
I WANT SWEET BUNS!
...
SHCH~
HWOO
SKFF
FIVE-SECOND RULE...
GRIN
TK
TK

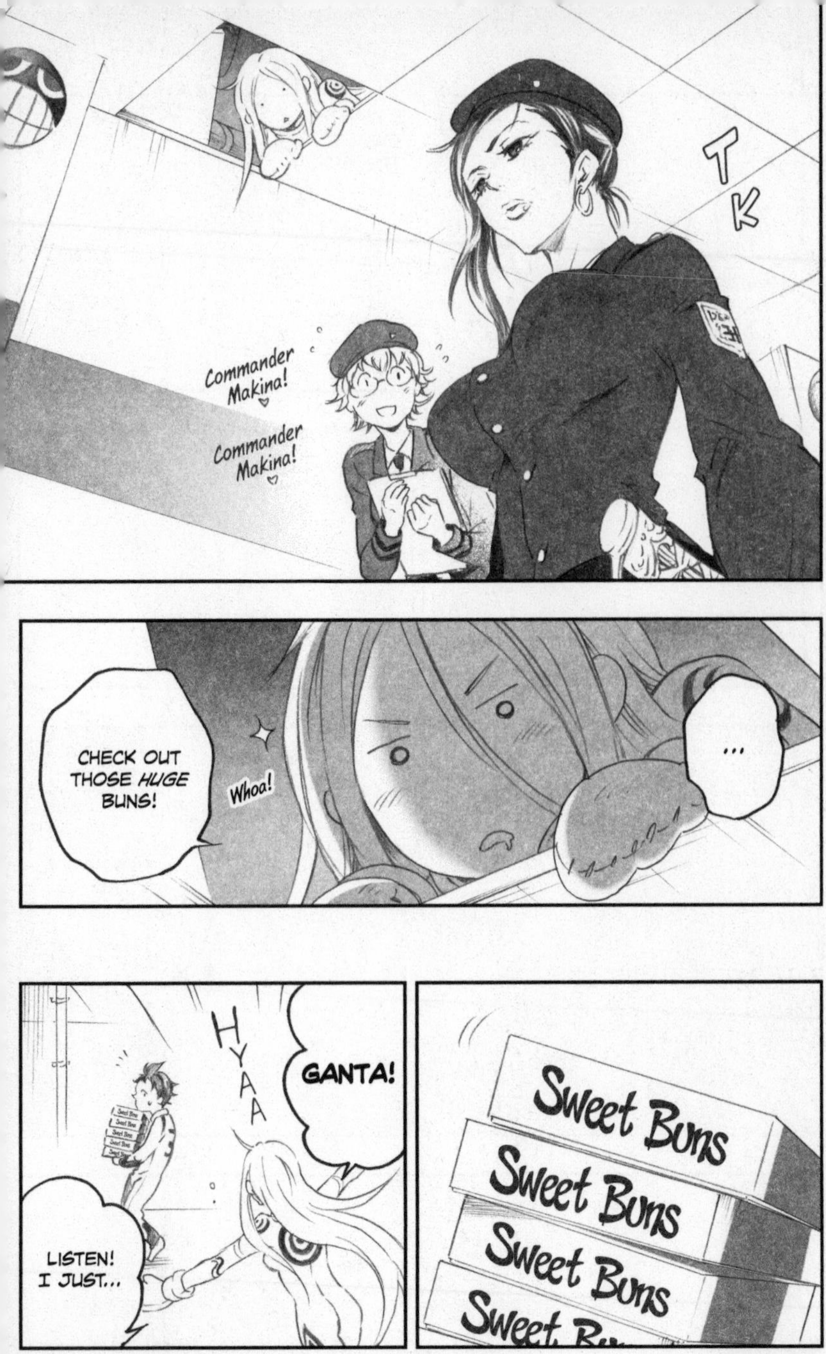
TK
Commander Makina!
Commander Makina!
...
Whoa!
CHECK OUT THOSE HUGE BUNS!
Sweet Buns
Sweet Buns
Sweet Buns
GANTA!
HYAA
LISTEN! I JUST...

HUH ?!
WHY DO YOU HAVE ...
...A BUN ON YOUR HEAD ?!
...
IT'S A PUNISHMENT BECAUSE OF YOU!
THIS PLACE REALLY SUCKS.
...
SIGH
I'M SORRY.

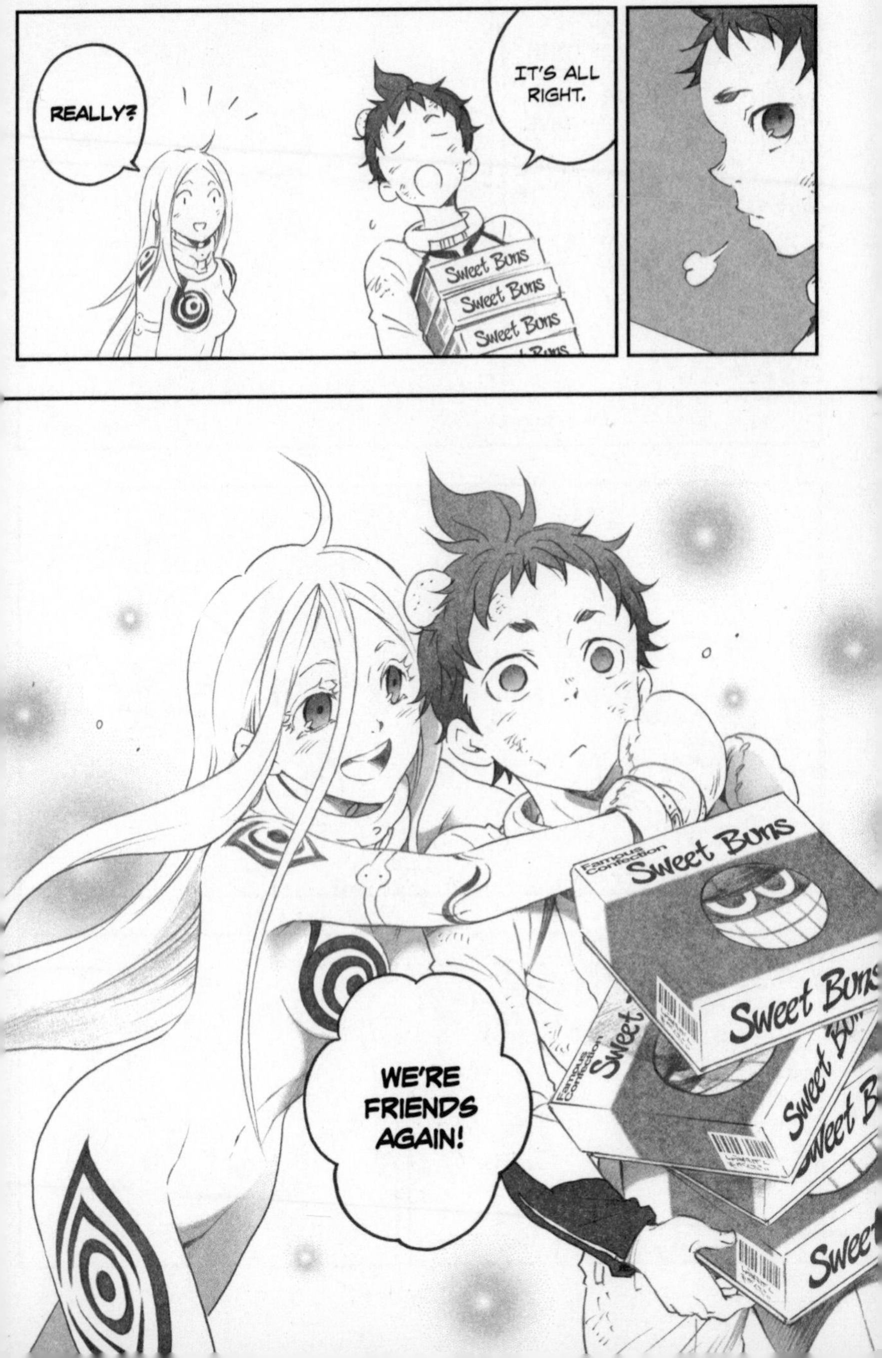
IT'S ALL RIGHT.
REALLY?
Sweet Buns
Sweet Buns
Sweet Buns
Famous Confection Sweet Buns
WE'RE FRIENDS AGAIN!
Sweet Buns

SO LET'S EAT THESE BUNS TOGETHER!
There's so many!
Hey!
NO! YOU CAN'T!
Sweet Buns
It's not all bad.
The End

DEADMAN WONDERLAND Extra 2

MY NAME IS YO TAKAMI.
MY LITTLE SISTER, MINATSUKI. SHE'S SO ADORABLE.
MMMPH
Ganta, you %#$¢...
THAT'S RIGHT, I CAME TO DEADMAN WONDERLAND TO PROTECT MY LITTLE SISTER!
DUN

YAWN
SHE'S EVEN CUTE WHEN SHE'S GRUMPY IN THE MORNING...
GOOD MORNING, MINATSUKI.
I'D BE HAPPY TO HELP YOU FRESHEN UP.
If you just untied me a little?
JAB
LOSE THE LIGHT.
MY EYES! MY EYES!

SHE'S CUTE WHEN SHE'S SHOPPING...
TWO DOUBLE CHEESE-BURGERS AND A SALAD.
A TERIYAKI AVOCADO BURGER MEAL...
...WITH A MILK TEA.
?!
YOU'RE ORDERING TOO MUCH.
AS YOUR BROTHER, I MUST HELP YOU WATCH YOUR FIGURE. ALSO...
...UPPING YOUR CALORIC INTAKE WON'T MAKE YOUR BOOBIES GROW...
KRAK
HERE YOU GO.
THANKS.

SHE'S CUTE WHEN SHE'S EATING...
STOP STARIN' AT ME WHILE I EAT.
You wanna lose the light again?
SWF
GURGLE
I'M KINDA HUNGRY...
BUT I LOST MY CP CARD WHEN I GOT TO G WARD...
Water's free, water's free...
WHEW... I'M STUFFED.

HEY, LOSER...
TAKE CARE OF THE LEFTOVERS, WILL YA?
BURGER FOOD
MINA-TSUKI!
YAAY
Hmph.
SHE'S CUTE WHEN SHE'S BEING KIND...

DEADMAN WONDERLAND
Extra 3

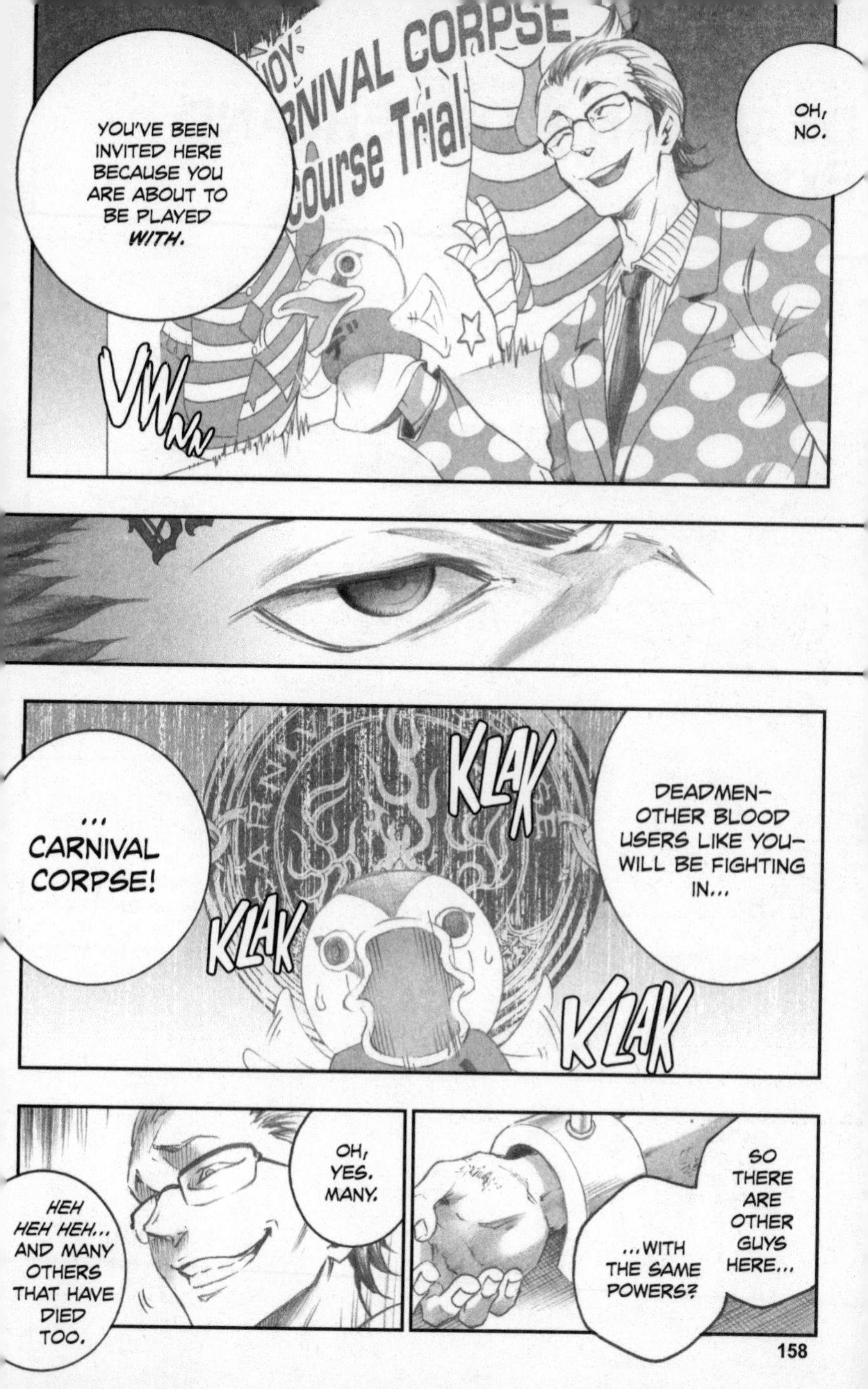
OH, NO.
YOU'VE BEEN INVITED HERE BECAUSE YOU ARE ABOUT TO BE PLAYED *WITH*.
CARNIVAL CORPSE
Course Trial
VWNN
DEADMEN— OTHER BLOOD USERS LIKE YOU— WILL BE FIGHTING IN...
... CARNIVAL CORPSE!
KLAK
KLAK
KLAK
SO THERE ARE OTHER GUYS HERE...
...WITH THE SAME POWERS?
OH, YES. MANY.
HEH HEH HEH... AND MANY OTHERS THAT HAVE DIED TOO.

YOU CANNOT SAY NO!
AND YOU CANNOT RUN AWAY!
KLAK
KLAK
KLAK
KLAK
YOU'RE GOING TO BE MY NEW TOY!
OH YEAH?
KLUNK

ADKT
KRIK
S-S-SLICE...
I'M THE ONE PLAYING THE GAMES.

DEADMAN WONDERLAND, EH?
MIGHT BE MY KINDA FUN.
ADKT

DEADMAN WONDERLAND Extra 4

MS. MAKINA ...
WHAT'RE YOU DOIN'?
?
I'M WORKING.
YER SUCH A HARD WORKER... ♡
HUU
?!
TINK
KASUGA... DON'T TELL ME YOU DRANK MY...
WOBBL
YOU MUST BE SO TIRED...
LET ME GIVE YOU A MASSAGE!
WOBBL
NO, I DON'T NEED ONE.

YOU MUST BE SO TIRED...
HEH HEH
LET ME GIVE YOU A MASSAGE!
*RINSE AND REPEAT
HEH HEH
...
I APPRECIATE THE THOUGHT.
BUT I HAVE A LOT OF WORK TO DO.
See all this?
TP TP
SWSH SWSH

YOU HAVE NO REASON TO SAY NO NOW.
SHING
Heh.
DONE
NO.
BUT... WHY?
SNF
IS IT BECAUSE I'M INEPT?
DON'T YOU LIKE ME?
IT'S NOT THAT...
HMMM
WAH
WIP
SWISH
WELL, IN THAT CASE...!
YOU'RE SO TENSE, MS. MAKINA! ♡
GR
AB
HEY! KASUGA?!
YOU'RE SO STIFF!
KNEAD
STOP! WHY ARE YOU UNDOING MY BRA?!
RELAX. I'LL BE GENTLE. ♡
FWIP
SEE, SEE, SEE, SEE?
RUB
SQUEEZE
STOP, DAMN IT!
AH!
KNEAD
RUB

SHNNG
KRAK
UNGH!
Justice has been served!
SHK
The next day...
COMMANDER MAKINA...
THROB
THROB
WHY ARE YOU SO ANGRY TODAY? Your aura... it's...
AND WHY DO MY HEAD AND NECK HURT?
NEXT TIME IT WON'T BE THE BLUNT SIDE OF THE SWORD.
??

DEADMAN WONDERLAND
Extra 5

IS IT JUST YOU IN HERE, NAGI?
I THOUGHT I HEARD A GIRL'S VOICE SINGING.
SWF
SWF
Y-YOU MUST BE MISTAKEN, KARAKO...
REALLY?
SKCH
SKCH
HMMM...
I CAN'T TELL HER I WAS PRACTICING USING MY ARTIFICIAL VOCAL CORDS TO MAKE A GIRL'S VOICE...

♪
DRRRRRN
YO, HIBANA...
HOW ABOUT A SONG TO LIGHTEN THINGS UP?
HMM...
HOW ABOUT ...
... "UNDER THE SPREADING CHESTNUT TREE"?

UNDER THE SPREADING ...
... CHESTNUT TREE... ♪
THERE WE SIT, BOTH YOU...
...AND ME... ♪
OH, HOW HAPPY... ♪
...WE WILL BE...
URGH!
THAT AIN'T ROCK 'N' ROLL!
BRNNNNG
GENKAKU! NO HEAD BANGING ALLOWED!

DEADMAN WONDERLAND
Extra 6

SWF
WHAT'RE YOU DOING, GANTA?!
FWP FWP
OH!
YAMA-KATSU! MIMI! I ALMOST HAD IT!
Had what?
C'mon, let's go!
Ah ha ha!
YOU'LL GET DETENTION IF YOU'RE LATE AGAIN!
WHATEVER.
LISTEN UP! I CAME TO VISIT YOU GUYS!
WAH
THAT'S RIGHT! I'M KOZUJI, THE TAE KWON DO CHAMP!

SNFL...
...
WAAAH
FWP
HEH...
?
AH HA HA HA HA HA
HEY! THEY STOLE OUR RATIONS AGAIN!
YOU'RE A COP... DO SOME-THING ABOUT IT!
Damn it
Hmm...
IT WAS JUST TWO PIECES OF BREAD...
WHAT'D YOU SAY?!
SORRY, SORRY.

TEAR
TOSS

DEADMAN WONDERLAND 12

Jinsei Kataoka
Kazuma Kondou

STAFF

Nao Ikegami
Karaiko
Shinji Sato
Taku Nakamura
Toshihiro Noguchi

CONTINUED IN VOLUME 13

DEADMAN WONDERLAND

DEADMAN WONDERLAND
VOLUME 12
VIZ MEDIA EDITION

STORY & ART BY
JINSEI KATAOKA, KAZUMA KONDOU

DEADMAN WONDERLAND VOLUME 12

EDITED BY KADOKAWA SHOTEN
FIRST PUBLISHED IN JAPAN IN 2013 BY KADOKAWA CORPORATION, TOKYO.
ENGLISH TRANSLATION RIGHTS ARRANGED WITH KADOKAWA CORPORATION, TOKYO.

TRANSLATION/JOE YAMAZAKI
ENGLISH ADAPTATION/STAN!
TOUCH-UP ART & LETTERING/JAMES GAUBATZ
DESIGN/SAM ELZWAY
EDITOR/JENNIFER LEBLANC

PRINTED IN THE U.S.A.

PUBLISHED BY VIZ MEDIA, LLC
P.O. BOX 77010
SAN FRANCISCO, CA 94107

10 9 8 7 6 5 4 3 2 1
FIRST PRINTING, DECEMBER 2015

www.viz.com